# Applied discourse analysis

## Social and psychological interventions

**EDITED BY CARLA WILLIG**

**Open University Press**
Buckingham · Philadelphia

In memory of Ben Heath,
who understood the limits of language

Open University Press
Celtic Court
22 Ballmoor
Buckingham
MK18 1XW

email: enquiries@openup.co.uk
world wide web: http://www.openup.co.uk

and
325 Chestnut Street
Philadelphia, PA 19106, USA

First published 1999

A catalogue record of this book is available from the British Library

ISBN 0 335 20226 8 (pbk)     0 335 20227 6 (hbk)

**Library of Congress Cataloging-in-Publication Data**
Applied discourse analysis: social and psychological interventions /
    edited by Carla Willig.
        p.    cm.
    Includes bibliographical references and index.
    ISBN 0-335-20227-6    ISBN 0-335-20226-8 (pbk)
    1. Psychology, Applied—Research—Methodology.  2. Discourse
analysis.  I. Willig, Carla. 1964–
    BF636.A595  1999
    401'.41–dc21                                    98–49829  CIP

Typeset by Graphicraft Limited, Hong Kong
Printed in Great Britain by Biddles Limited, Guildford and Kings Lynn

# Contents

# Notes on contributors

**Timothy Auburn** is a lecturer in the Department of Psychology at the University of Plymouth, where he teaches social and environmental psychology. His research interests include the social organization of police-suspect interviews and the use of discourse analysis in the evaluation of sex offender treatment programmes.

**Steven D. Brown** is a lecturer in social and organizational psychology at Keele University and a member of the Centre for Social Theory and Technology. He has published articles on the construction of stress, culture and technology, and the history and philosophy of psychology. He is currently investigating groupware and the mediation of memory within the ESRC Virtual Society programme.

**Susan Drake** has recently graduated from the DClinPsy course at the University of Exeter. Her research interests have focused on process-oriented evaluation of family therapy. A recent study has examined how silence is used communicatively within family therapy situations.

**Val Gillies** is undertaking her PhD research, which explores the discourses and constructions that mothers in non-traditional relationships draw on when discussing their children. She is also research fellow at Oxford Brookes

University and is currently working on a Joseph Rowntree funded project looking at the family lives of young people.

**David Harper** is Clinical Tutor/Practitioner at the University of Liverpool/ North Mersey Community Trust. He was co-author (with Ian Parker, Genie Georgaca, Terence McLoughlin and Mark Stowell-Smith) of *Deconstructing Psychopathology* and has recently completed a doctoral dissertation entitled 'Deconstructing paranoia: an analysis of the discourses associated with the concept of paranoid delusion'.

**Susan Lea** is a lecturer in the Department of Psychology at the University of Plymouth, where she teaches social psychology and health psychology. Her research interests include using discourse analysis in the evaluation of sex offender treatment programmes and the social construction of national identity.

**Joan Pujol** is Senior Lecturer at the Universitat Autonoma de Barcelona. He has been lecturer at the University of Huddersfield and Honorary Visiting Fellow at the University of Reading. His main topic of research has been the analysis of technoscientific discourse and his current research combines material and discursive perspectives in the analysis of social issues. He has published journal articles and book chapters on these topics and he is co-author of *The Non-delinquents: How Citizens Understand Criminality* (with P. Garcia-Boros, M. Cagius, J. C. Medina and J. Sanchez), which won a Spanish national research award.

**Carla Willig** is Lecturer in Psychology at City University. Her research is concerned with the relationship between discourse and practice, particularly in relation to risk-taking. She has published journal articles and book chapters on the discursive construction of trust and sexual safety, and she has contributed to the debate about relativism and realism in social constructionist psychology.

# Foreword

Recent years have seen a transformation in the social sciences and in the language that researchers use to make sense of action and experience. This transformation has also opened up a space in academic institutions for reflexive questioning about what that language does in the world. Critical research on discourse, text and the social construction of things that were once taken for granted has inspired work across the disciplines, including cultural studies, psychology, sociology and human geography. It is now time to take stock of what we have accomplished and where we are going with this work, and so these three books review social constructionist perspectives in order to explore new ground creatively.

We accomplish three things: produce a clear theoretical overview of social constructionist frameworks; move our understanding of textuality beyond language; and embed analysis of discourse in an account of practice. There is a different emphasis in each book: Nightingale and Cromby's *Social Constructionist Psychology* surveys existing work and gathers together critical reflections on the conditions and limits of research on language; Parker and the Bolton Discourse Network's *Critical Textwork* elaborates and extends the compass of research to many kinds of textual domain; and Willig's *Applied Discourse Analysis* consistently and provocatively asks through a range of examples how such research can be made useful.

There are fruitful overlaps, with examples of discourse analysis, discussions of types of text and theoretical reflections on the social construction of meaning in each. Together the books address different facets of a common task – they take forward critical social constructionist research on discursive practice.

*Ian Parker*
*Professor of Psychology*
*Bolton Institute*

# Acknowledgements

I would like to thank the British Academy for financial support in the early stages of this project. A British Academy award facilitated the organization and presentation of a Symposium on Applied Discourse Analysis at the Fourth European Congress of Psychology in Athens, Greece, in the summer of 1995. I would also like to thank the School of Social Science, Middlesex University, for a publications grant which allowed me to complete this book on time.

# **1** **Introduction:** making a difference

## CARLA WILLIG

This book is about the relationship between discourse analytic work and applied psychology. The aim of the book is to examine critically the contribution discourse analytic studies can make to processes of social and psychological change. The book is motivated by the desire to move beyond critical commentary and towards an active engagement with social and political practice. However, it is important to acknowledge that the relationship between critical analysis and progressive practice is by no means unproblematic. Indeed, one of the reasons for discourse analysts' reluctance to move beyond critical commentary has been an acute awareness of the dangers associated with a clear commitment to particular policies and practices. This chapter: (a) introduces and problematizes both discourse analysis and applied psychology; (b) reviews three major critiques of applied psychology; and (c) critically reviews three ways in which discourse analysts have attempted to engage with social and political practice to date. The chapter concludes by introducing the contributions which constitute the main body of this book.

### Discourse analysis in psychology

In recent years discourse analysis has become an increasingly popular research tool in psychology (e.g. Potter and Wetherell 1987; Edwards and

Potter 1992; Parker 1992; Burman and Parker 1993; Burr 1995). Discourse analysis is concerned with the ways in which language constructs objects, subjects and experiences, including subjectivity and a sense of self. Discourse analysts conceptualize language as constitutive of experience rather than representational or reflective. They argue that the linguistic categories we use in order to 'describe' reality are not in fact reflections of intrinsic and defining features of entities. Instead, they bring into being the objects they describe. Furthermore, there is always more than one way of describing something and our choice of how to use words to package perceptions and experiences gives rise to particular versions of events and of reality. It is in this sense that language can be said to construct reality. Discourse analysis, therefore, provides a clear alternative to the categorization of behaviours, measurement of variables and attempts to develop predictive models of human behaviour, which constitute mainstream psychology. Discourse analysis is attractive to many psychologists because it allows the researcher to problematize the categories used in mainstream psychology. For example, discourse analysts have used their method to deconstruct emotions (e.g. Harré 1986; Stenner 1993), prejudice (e.g. Potter and Wetherell 1987; Wetherell and Potter 1992), psychopathology (Parker *et al*. 1995), trust (Willig 1997) and the psychological subject itself (e.g. Henriques *et al*. 1984; Hollway 1989). These studies explore the ways in which particular categories are constructed and used, and with what consequences. Something like 'trust', for example, ceases to be conceptualized as a stable trait or as a set of cognitions residing within the individual's mind; instead, 'trust' is seen as situationally specific, negotiated and purposeful social action. The researcher explores how 'trust' is talked about, in what contexts and by whom, and what social or interpersonal objectives may be achieved through its deployment. In addition, discourse analysis allows the researcher to identify subject positions which may constrain or facilitate particular actions and experiences. For example, a biomedical discourse offers the subject positions of 'doctor' and 'patient', each of which prescribes certain practices and proscribes others. Being positioned as 'the patient', for instance, involves granting strangers access to one's passive body. Discourse analysis is an attractive research tool for critical psychologists because it allows us to question and challenge dominant constructions of psychologically relevant concepts (e.g. 'mental illness', 'intelligence', 'personality'). By deconstructing such categories, we can demonstrate that things could be different, that our customary ways of categorizing and ordering phenomena are reified and interest-driven rather than simple reflections of 'reality'. By revealing the constructed nature of psychological phenomena, we create a space for making available alternatives to what has become psychological common sense.

There are a number of different approaches to discourse analysis in psychology. Potter and Wetherell (1995) differentiate between a focus on discourse practices, i.e. a concern with what people do with their talk and writing (i.e. the action orientation of discourse), and a focus on the discursive resources that people draw on (i.e. interpretive repertoires or discourses). The latter focus derives from the work of Foucault and has been more popular outside psychology (e.g. cultural studies and medical sociology, but see Parker 1992; Parker *et al.* 1995 for such work in psychology); the former draws on Sacks's (1992) work in conversation analysis and is now widely used within psychology (e.g. Potter and Wetherell 1987; Edwards and Potter 1992). Both approaches, however, are used to address psychological concerns. A focus on discourse practices allows us to study psychological activities such as remembering and making attributions (see Edwards and Potter 1992), while a focus on discursive resources allows us to explore the role of discourse in the construction of objects and subjects, including the 'self' (e.g. Hollway 1989; Crawford *et al.* 1992; Parker *et al.* 1995). (See also Widdicombe and Woofitt 1995, and Burr 1995, for a discussion of different approaches to discourse analysis in psychology.) While discourse analysis has generally been concerned with written or spoken words, it can also be used in order to produce critical readings of other forms of text. In *Critical Textwork*, Parker (1999) argues that discourse may be studied wherever there is meaning. This includes visual (e.g. comics, flags) and physical (e.g. cities, bodies) texts. *Critical Textwork* provides a comprehensive introduction to the ways in which discourse analysis can open up different forms of text to a critical reading.

Given that many discourse analysts in psychology use their method in order to challenge the categories which constitute the starting point for mainstream psychology and in order to draw attention to the flexibility of social and personal being, we might expect them to have something to say about how things could be different. For example, if a discourse of psychopathology and its associated practices and institutions serves to disempower users of mental health services (e.g. Parker *et al.* 1995), then how can this be changed? Are there ways of talking about emotional distress which are preferable? And how can such alternative constructions and practices be promoted? On the whole, discourse analysts have been reluctant to move beyond deconstruction and to make recommendations for improved social and psychological practice. There are a number of very powerful arguments supporting such reluctance and these are discussed later in this chapter. However, before we move into a discussion of the problematic relationship between discourse analytic research and its potential application, it is necessary to introduce the concept of applied psychology.

## Applied psychology

The *Penguin Dictionary of Psychology* (1982: 18) describes applied psychology as 'the branch of psychology which seeks to apply to practical problems and practical life the methods and results of pure, and especially experimental psychology'. However, it is difficult to find an explicit definition of applied psychology by those who advocate its practice. Authors tend either to review critically different approaches to the practice of applied psychology (e.g. Howitt 1991) or to assume that the concept is unproblematic and self-explanatory and does not require an explicit definition (e.g. Semin and Fiedler 1996). For example, a recent collection of papers entitled *Applied Social Psychology* (Semin and Fiedler 1996) does not include an introductory chapter outlining the editors' conceptualization of the discipline (or a discussion of whether applied psychology is indeed a discipline), nor does it conclude by discussing the various contributors' approaches to the notion of application in relation to one another. This absence indicates an assumed consensus as to the nature of applied psychology. Upon reading the preface as well as the 15 chapters which make up Semin and Fiedler's (1996) collection, it is possible to extract the editors' conceptualization of what it means to apply psychology: applied social psychology refers to the use of existing social psychological theories, generally derived from laboratory experiments, in order to explain real world phenomena, such as social events and processes. Recommendations for appropriate social and psychological interventions are made on the basis of these theories. Thus, a successful intervention would be one which manipulates relevant variables, as specified by a particular social psychological theory, in order to achieve a specified outcome. The kinds of questions being asked by applied social psychologists in the volume are as follows. Why do people engage in certain behaviours (e.g. health-impairing practices, risky driving, aggression)? Why do certain social processes take the course that they do (e.g. group dynamics in organizations, political movements)? What are the effects of particular social and cognitive contexts on individual and group behaviours? Finally, what can be done in order to manipulate, influence and change these social psychological processes? The book selects a number of theoretical frameworks as being particularly pertinent to applied settings. These include: the relationship between attitudes and behaviour, as theorized by Ajzen and Fishbein (1980) and Ajzen (1988); cognitive theories of judgement and decision-making; and the role of language as a strategic tool in social interaction. Thus, two assumptions characterize this book's conceptualization of applied psychology. First, the movement of knowledge is unidirectional in that it is transferred from the academic research setting (e.g. the psychological laboratory) to the 'real world', but not vice versa. Second, there is a clear split between the 'real world' and the realm where knowledge is produced. So, for example, Chapter 4 is devoted to a discussion of 'Language in Applied Contexts', which suggests that there is such a thing as pure language which can be studied outside of real-life contexts.

Potter (1982: 23) develops the argument that there is a mismatch between what he calls 'the ideology of application' and the way in which social psychological theory actually informs practice. The ideology of application 'suggests a continuum of research from "pure" to "applied" with knowledge "flowing" from one end to the other' (Potter 1982: 24). In addition, it is suggested that scientific theories receive validation through their successful application. In reality, Potter argues, the two spheres (theory/science versus practice/technology) are institutionally and intellectually separate. They have their own separate literatures and conferences, and innovations tend to develop within each area. In addition, the vast majority of social psychological research is (potentially) applicable as opposed to (actually) applied. Potter also draws attention to the situated nature of scientific theories and their application, whereby institutional, social, political and economic interests influence the process of application. Thus, Potter (1982: 47) differentiates between an idealized conception of 'application' and the realities of application, and concludes that it is by no means clear 'whether our discipline is really the positive and critical social force that many would like'.

Howitt (1991) acknowledges the many shortcomings of and dangers associated with applied psychology. He points out that 'many of the ways in which psychology is "applied" seem trivial, crude, inappropriate, and even disgraceful' (Howitt 1991: 1); however, he concludes that this does not mean that psychologists should relinquish their commitment to positive social change. He argues that 'psychology should seek to have something to offer society on the significant problems facing it' (Howitt 1991: 148). Howitt observes that even though there are numerous publications in the area of applied psychology (e.g. clinical, educational and prison psychology), few attempts have been made to develop a systematic, theory-oriented account of the process of applying psychology. This is, in part, a result of the pure–applied distinction (as referred to by Potter 1982) and the assumption that the movement from pure to applied work is smooth and unproblematic. However, Howitt reminds us that the most influential psychological 'technologies', such as intelligence, ability, aptitude and personality testing as well as psychotherapy, are largely atheoretical. Howitt characterizes existing 'applied psychology' as the application of psychological methods of research in real-world (i.e. non-laboratory) settings (rather than the application of basic theory to real-world situations) and proposes the more appropriate label 'real-life' research. In Chapter 2 of his book, Howitt (1991: 15) discusses ways in which the nature of the discipline of psychology itself prevents 'the development of a fully-fledged, worldly psychology'. For example, the search for universal laws of human behaviour and the retention of the laboratory experiment as the central research methodology constitute a major obstacle to what Howitt describes as 'real-world psychology' (*ibid.*). A Cartesian positivist approach to science encourages an 'unfettered quest for knowledge' (Howitt 1991: 22) by removing the need to justify socially or morally one's choice of the object of study.

According to this approach, the 'truth' is out there, and it is the scientist's task to discover as much of it as possible. Howitt argues that a social constructionist approach has much to offer to a psychology of social issues. This is because social constructionism abandons positivism's concern with a fixed reality to be discovered and instead, and here Howitt quotes Gergen, 'attempts to articulate common forms of understanding as they now exist, as they have existed in prior historical periods, and as they might exist should creative attention be so directed' (Gergen 1985: 266, in Howitt 1991: 29–30). Thus, the choice of what to study, how and for what purposes cannot be separated from the knowledge that is being created in the process. Consequently, any contribution to a body of knowledge is always also a recommendation about how things should or should not be. Despite this close connection between social constructionist research and change, social constructionist researchers have not been involved in 'applying' their work. In Howitt's words, social constructionism offers the 'possibility of creating previously unimagineable views of people and society'; however, 'this challenge has not begun to be met' (Howitt 1991: 33).

## Action research and community psychology

There is, of course, a psychological tradition of active involvement in social change. Action research has been a distinctive form of social enquiry since the 1940s (see Hart and Bond 1995). Beginning with Kurt Lewin's work, action research has developed into a number of different approaches in recent years. Action research means to 'study things through changing them' (Banister *et al.* 1994: 108). Lewin was interested in understanding and solving social problems such as the growth of authoritarianism, low morale among the American military in the Second World War and anti-semitism. His main concern was with the nature of group dynamics, and he believed in the possibility of change through 'rational social management' (Lewin 1946: 206). However, Lewin has been criticized for putting his ideas at the disposal of powerful elites (e.g. the US government, factory bosses) (e.g. van Elteren 1992) without questioning their objectives and without taking the interests of the subjects of the research (e.g. soldiers, workers) into account. In recent years, and as a response to such concerns with power relations, new forms of action research have emerged (see Carr and Kemmis 1986). Participatory action research differs from the Lewinian approach in that the participants become genuine collaborators of the researcher. They are involved in all stages of the research process, including the identification of the 'problem' or research question. Action research is not seen as a form of re-education of the participants or as social engineering, but rather as empowerment. Here, applying psychology is not about using psychological knowledge derived from laboratory research in order to manipulate real-life situations, and it is not about applying psychological research methods in real-world settings. Rather, it is about finding participant-led ways of improving specific problematic social situations. The psychologist's role in this is to facilitate this process by making available to participants the use of data gathering and analysis skills. However, action research is not a popular research tool in psychology, and we have to look to other disciplines (e.g. education, organizational studies, nursing) to find examples of participatory action research projects (see Hart and Bond 1995).

Community psychology (e.g. Levine and Perkins 1987; Orford 1992) refers to a way of applying psychology which shares some features with action research. It is concerned with practising psychology outside of institutions such as clinics, schools and penal establishments. Community psychology aims to empower (potential) service users by involving them in problem identification and the search for solutions. It is opposed to an individualistic approach to psychological issues, instead preferring to intervene at a number of levels, including social, societal, political and individual. As a result, community psychology cannot be isolated from political and social activism. However, at the same time, community psychology remains committed to systematic research and theory-building. According to Orford:

> Community Psychology is an applied subject. In other words, it is a practical subject, concerning itself with trying to change things at one or more level, from micro to macro. But it is a branch of psychology, and it is therefore as thoroughly committed to the building up of theory and knowledge through research, and the sound evaluation of practice, as are all other branches of psychology.
>
> Orford (1992: 8)

Community psychology is a branch of applied psychology which attempts to avoid some of the ethical and political problems associated with a social engineering perspective.

**Problems with application**

There are a number of ways in which the idea of applying psychology has been criticized, both from within and from outside mainstream psychology. The major criticism from within the discipline refers to the twin dangers of 'bias' and 'politics'. It is argued that psychologists who are called upon to provide scientific evidence to policy-makers are in danger of becoming motivated by their own values and political commitments. Howitt (1991: 35) quotes Atkinson (1977: 207–8), who argues that 'psychologists and other social scientists . . . need to carefully distinguish between providing scientific data and making policy . . . Otherwise, psychology will come to be regarded as a social force rather than a scientific discipline.' Discourse analysts, whose approach to research is, after all, based upon a direct challenge to mainstream psychology's claims to scientific objectivity, do not share Atkinson's concerns about bias. From a social constructionist point of view, all knowledge-talk has an action orientation. This is because even communication about 'facts' takes place within a particular social context. What we say or write (about) constitutes a contribution to an ongoing social debate, and it has social consequences. We do not simply state what is the case (e.g. that the table is round) unless there is a (potential) claim that it may not be so (see Billig 1987). It follows that even scientific observations cannot be detached and uninvolved. Instead of futile attempts to avoid 'bias', social constructionist psychology (ideally) includes a reflexive analysis of the researcher's standpoint and perspective, as well as the (social, cultural, historical) context within which the research takes place (see also Burr 1995: 160–2). Consequently, the risk of 'bias' is not an obstacle to discourse analysts' involvement with applied psychology. However, there are powerful arguments against such involvement. Three major challenges can be identified: these are concerned with the ideology of application, the abuse of power and processes of reification. Each will be discussed in turn.

### The ideology of application critique

Potter's (1982) argument, outlined earlier, exposes the mismatch between the ideology and the reality of application. The former serves to obscure the latter, by failing to acknowledge the situated nature of all knowledge. According to Potter, the institutional context of science, wider social, political and economic contexts and the interests of the participants (including the scientists) all contribute to the ways in which psychological theories are actually applied. For example, psychological theories can be used to legitimate an application which has been undertaken for socio-economic reasons. The ideology of application, therefore, is a way of mystifying and thus legitimizing particular interest-driven applications. By claiming that application is a smooth process of simply applying objective knowledge discovered in the laboratory to real-world situations, the ideology of application silences any potential questions about how, why and in whose interests psychological theories are being applied.

### The abuse/power critique

Cromby and Standen (1996) argue that the current government squeeze on funding in the UK means that an increasing amount of research funding is directed at finding solutions for social problems. The definition of what constitutes a social problem is provided by those who are providing the research funding. For example, the UK *Health of the Nation* report of 1992 focused upon healthy eating and a reduction in smoking prevalence in order to improve health. Within this context, psychological research can become a resource to promote healthy living. However, by accepting a focus upon individual behaviour change as opposed to the effects of poverty and unemployment on life expectancy, morbidity and mortality, psychologists 'however unwittingly are helping to conceal a much bigger risk to health' (Cromby and Standen 1996: 7). Further, psychological research findings have been used to justify changes in patient care which are in reality a response to financial pressures. For example, psychological research has been used to justify early discharge from hospital as well as care in the community policies, both of which are primarily motivated by economic considerations, and both of which have detrimental consequences for carers, especially those who are economically disadvantaged. Cromby and Standen's (1996) critique of applied psychology focuses on the ways in which psychological research findings can easily be (ab)used by governments and other powerful groups in the pursuit of political and/or economic objectives.

## The reification critique

Widdicombe (1995) is concerned with more subtle manifestations of power. She draws attention to the ways in which social scientists' accounts can be intended to liberate oppressed groups but end up by simply locking them within different restrictive discourses. Widdicombe (1995) draws attention to the dangers of reification. She advises critical psychologists against committing themselves to particular recommendations for interventions. Instead, she argues that the best way to avoid imposing categories of meaning upon others is to stick to contextualized analysis and not to generalize from one's research findings. This allows respondents to redefine themselves and their experiences each time they are studied by researchers. According to Widdicombe (1995), giving respondents this space is more empowering for respondents than any progressive policy recommendations.

## The implications of these three critiques for discourse analysts who want to make a difference

At worst, they lead us to the conclusion that getting involved with interventions is so risky and so fraught with difficulties that it is best avoided. At best, they draw attention to a number of dangers associated with application which are serious but which can be circumvented. There are not many discourse analysts who have taken up the question of application, and fewer still who have attempted to formulate concrete proposals for social and psychological interventions. Existing discourse analytic attempts to address social and political practice take three forms: Discourse analysis as social critique, discourse analysis as empowerment and discourse analysis as guide to reform. These are not, however, mutually exclusive approaches. For example, discourse analysis as social critique forms part of both discourse analysis as empowerment and discourse analysis as guide to reform. Each approach is introduced, illustrated and critically evaluated below.

## Discourse analysis as social critique

Discourse analysis as social critique is concerned with exposing the ways in which language conspires to legitimate and perpetuate unequal power relations. For example, in *Mapping the Language of Racism*, Wetherell and Potter (1992) explore the discursive practice of racism through an analysis of a corpus of interviews with Pakeha New Zealanders. They use discourse analysis 'as a method of social critique' by showing 'how colonial history and current forms of Maori disadvantage are justified and rationalized, how inequality is normalized and rendered "safe", and how diversity and continuing conflicts are subdued and consensus manufactured' (Wetherell and Potter 1992: 115).

They invoke Foucault's argument that one way to undermine a 'truth' is not to counterpose it with another 'truth' but to examine the discursive processes by which true and false statements become distinguished. Wetherell and Potter deconstruct notions such as race, culture and nation as they are used in respondents' accounts, which allows them to identify among their respondents a collectively shared set of resources for legitimating their social position. They argue that

> from our perspective, then, an important part of anti-racist practice is identifying the forms legitimation takes, and charting also the fragmented and dilemmatic nature of everyday discourse, because it is at those points of fracture and contradiction that there is scope for change and the redirection of argument.
>
> (Wetherell and Potter 1992: 219)

Another example of discourse analysis as social critique is Wilkinson and Kitzinger's (1995) *Feminism and Discourse: Psychological Perspectives*. The book is in two parts ('Empirical work' and 'Theoretical advances'), reflecting the editors' twin objectives of illustrating the application of the discourse analytic method to 'a range of feminist topics', and critically evaluating discourse analysis in relation to 'the feminist project of intellectual, social and political change' (Wilkinson and Kitzinger 1995: 7). It is argued that discourse analysis can improve our understanding of the ways in which discursive practices position women, how gendered subjectivities are constituted and what their consequences are for women's experience. The empirical chapters trace the ways in which discursive constructions and practices shape women's experiences of menstruation, sexual harassment, being 'women' (and children) and anorexia nervosa. All aim to expose the role of discourse in the perpetuation of women's oppression and/or pathologization. The theoretical chapters debate the question of political and/or value commitments and their role in feminist discourse analysis.

Discourse analysis as social critique uses exposure through publication as its method of intervention. The workings of language and their socio-political and personal consequences are problematized and scrutinized, a process which, it is hoped, will facilitate progressive personal and social change. Armed with the insights of discourse analytic work, readers of such literature are in a better position to resist and challenge dominant (and oppressive) discursive constructions. Discourse as social critique does not, however, spell out how such resistance and challenge may be put into practice. Wetherell and Potter (1992: 220) take care to point out that discourse should not be the sole site for action in relation to racism, and that a combination of 'critique and local action around specific issues' is to be recommended. However, they do not address the relationship between discursive critique and social action. What types of local action are we to take? To what extent can discourse analytic research inform such actions? And what are the effects of such action on discourse? Discourse analysis as social critique and socio-political interventions coexist but remain conceptually and practically independent and separate. Likewise, Wilkinson and Kitzinger's (1995) collection does not address the relationship between discourse analysis and social intervention. For example, Lovering's (1995) chapter criticizes contemporary sex education for failing to take into account cultural meanings surrounding sexuality. However, having analysed adolescent girls' and boys' talk about menstruation, she does not formulate recommendations for improved sex education practice. Similarly, Kitzinger and Thomas (1995) analyse the mechanisms through which sexual harrassment is constructed and managed. Again, the authors do not move beyond improved understanding as a goal of their research. Indeed, they criticize existing attempts (e.g. codes of practice or legislation) to tackle sexual harrassment in the workplace by claiming that these cannot change what are complex social relations and practices, and argue that

> what is needed instead is an understanding and deconstruction of the discursive techniques used to render sexual harrassment invisible or non-existent, and an understanding of how it is that the 'victims' of sexual harrassment are themselves complicit in this process.
>
> (Kitzinger and Thomas 1995: 46)

No discussion is offered as to how (or whether) such understanding can lead to change.

To summarize, discourse analysis as social critique promotes exposure through publication as a form of resistance. Although not (necessarily) hostile to intervention, discourse analysis as social critique does not theorize the relationship between discursive critique and social intervention. It does not enable us to use our discourse analytic research findings in order to develop strategic interventions such as anti-racist campaigns, sex education programmes or action against sexual harrassment.

## Discourse analysis as empowerment

Discourse analysis as empowerment is concerned with the identification of counter-discourses. Deconstruction and critique of dominant discourses and practices of regulation are followed by an exploration of alternative accounts and positionings. Empowerment is sought through the promotion of subversive discursive practices and spaces of resistance. For example, Burman *et al.* (1996) use discourse perspectives in order to analyse psychology's role in the legitimation of social inequalities. However, the authors distance themselves from deconstructive work which is 'concerned with critique rather than the production of alternative constructions' (Burman 1996: 6). Instead, the objective of the book is to identify opportunities for active resistance inside and outside of institutions. Chapters in the book explore the ways in which psychological discourses and practices construct the subjects they regulate within the contexts of self-help, educational psychology, feminist therapy, mental health services, child-rearing, the media and gender identity clinics. All chapters identify spaces for resistance either through the subversive use of psychological discourse (e.g. when the technology of psychological testing is used to resist the pathologization of children's behaviour) or through the use of counter-discourses (e.g. when people choose to retain their ambiguous sexual/gender identities within gender-reassignment programmes). The authors are committed to localized resistance rather than globalizing strategies. This is because, the authors argue, it is the contextualized and strategic uses of discourses by powerful elites which are oppressive rather than the discourses themselves.

Parker *et al.* (1995) take a similar approach to the question of intervention. Their book aims to do three things: first, to deconstruct the discourses and practices of psychopathology; second, to explore their implications for subjective experience and treatment; third, to promote alternative accounts which can inform improved mental health practice. The authors identify six oppositions around which most psychiatric diagnoses are constructed. They include the individual and the social; reason and unreason; pathology and normality; form and content; pure categories versus messy real life; professional versus 'lay' views. Through a deconstruction of these binaries, the authors are able to challenge essentialist claims and to explore how politics and power are implicated in the construction of psychiatric categories. The book moves beyond the presentation of a critique of traditional psychiatric discourse and practice by drawing the reader's attention to contemporary campaigns against oppressive practices as well as existing alternative forms of mental health practice. The two major alternatives discussed are deconstructive therapy (e.g. narrative therapy) and the Hearing Voices Network (HVN). Narrative therapy (e.g. Epston and White 1989) involves the externalization and objectification of the problem (e.g. the diagnosis of schizophrenia) through a process of questioning. Such questioning includes an exploration of the role of the expert in defining the patient's experience. Deconstructive therapy treats 'the problem' (rather than the patient) as the problem and therefore constitutes a challenge to the traditional role of the expert (therapist, psychologist, psychiatrist etc.). The HVN provides a space where areas of experience (such as hearing voices) can be redefined outside the psychiatric apparatus. Here, voice hearing is conceptualized as an aspect of personal development which can be coped with in a variety of ways. The focus is upon the content of the voices as opposed to the fact of their existence. In other words, they are not perceived to be a symptom of some underlying disorder but as a facet of human experience which forms part of the hearer's reality. HVN self-help groups develop ways of living with the voices. The book concludes by providing a list of addresses of groups and organizations which have an activist and campaigning focus and which the reader may wish to contact in order to put the ideas introduced in the book into practice.

Discourse analysis as empowerment directly addresses the question of application. Discourse analysts who adopt this approach identify and promote discursive strategies for resistance. Discourse analysis as empowerment promotes action at a grass-roots level rather than top-down interventions, and it promotes organizations which facilitate such resistance. Here, discourse analysis serves as a method of social critique but it is also a tool to bring about social change. Discourse analysts, however, differ in the extent to which they are prepared to formulate specific recommendations for intervention and/or practice. Some, such as Burman et al. (1996), are highly suspicious of concrete and specific advice. They point out that, 'rather than making specific recommendations or prefigure specific interventions, we challenge the assumptions that have structured the terrain of the "psy complex", and thus render it open to new possibilities' (Burman 1996: 7). Others, such as Parker et al. (1995), are prepared to recommend specific, existing projects and practices such as deconstructive therapy and the HVN. However, this position is softened by the authors' insistence that 'it is the diversity of critique that gives it strength' (Parker et al. 1995: 132) and by their concern to distance themselves from global truth claims. Thus, support for interventions is always provisional and tactical, rather than final and absolute.

There are two problems with a commitment to diversity and its reluct-ance to replace one truth claim with another. First, it does not take into account the long-term effects of localized interventions. A particular dis-course may be used within a specific context in order to advance the interests of the oppressed in the short term. By mobilizing this discourse, however, we may legitimize and perpetuate oppressive institutional practices which are bound up with this discourse. For example, in the later stages of the anti-apartheid struggle in South Africa, critical psychologists were confronted with the question of whether or not psychologists ought to appear as expert witnesses in political trials. An effective defence could be, and was on occasion, that the accused had been subject to deindividuation and other social psychological processes, and that they were consequently not responsible for violent actions carried out within a crowd setting (Colman 1994). However, the use of psychological discourse in order to save anti-apartheid activists from the death penalty simultaneously under-mined the anti-apartheid struggle in the long term because it pathologized the collectivity of protestors by attributing their actions to psychological mechanisms rather than to the specific history of the conflict and the political objectives of participants (see Reicher 1994). A similar example is the use of premenstrual syndrome in the defence of a battered woman who has killed her violent husband. The mobilization of a biomedical discourse which pathologizes women may be in the interest of the accused woman, but it is also going to prop up discrimination against women in society as a whole. The argument that discourses are not either 'good' or 'bad' for oppressed groups but that their effects are entirely localized and contextual can lead to opportunistic uses of dominant discourses which ultimately do not benefit the struggle against oppression.

Second, an emphasis on diversity and flexibility can be disempowering and paralysing. Discourse analysis as empowerment assumes that deconstruc-tion of monolithic truths and awareness of contextualized complexities and alternative readings is liberating. For example, Allwood (1996: 35) argues that 'it might help someone experiencing being depressed to know that the cause(s) of their distress is (are) not known', because this would allow him or her to choose a personal and contingent interpretation of the depression. Similarly, Alldred (1996) suggests that tensions between discourses of child-rearing afford an opportunity for localized resistance and that it is not advisable to promote one particular approach to child-rearing (such as a feminist one) as an alternative to more traditional ones. I would argue that being faced with a proliferation of alternative and often conflicting accounts of the causes and consequences of particular processes and experiences can be profoundly disorientating. This is particularly the case for people who are undergoing a life crisis such as ill health or emotional distress, and for those whose actions have important consequences for the well-being of others (such as children). Being faced with choices in the absence of any criteria for making such choices can undermine our ability to act. In addition, if resistance can only be localized and contextualized, it follows that most of the time individuals will be on their own, or in very small groups, when faced with the need, and the opportunity, to resist in a particular way. If strategies of resistance cannot be generalized across contexts and across people, how can large numbers of people adopt a common strategy of resistance? And this is, of course, what is needed in order to achieve significant and lasting social change. To summarize, discourse as empowerment seeks to identify spaces for resistance to dominant discourses. It promotes counter-discourses and subversive discursive practices. However, even though it advocates collective and organized forms of resistance, its emphasis upon diversity and its commitment to localized resistance can fragment and therefore disempower those who wish to achieve lasting social change.

## Discourse analysis as guide to reform

Discourse analysis as guide to reform is praxis-oriented in that it seeks to use the results of discourse analytic studies in order to develop social interventions. Discourse analysis as guide to reform is committed to radical social change but it does not limit its recommendations to action from below. Instead, discourse analysts who adopt this approach also formulate proposals for improved practice within existing institutions, such as schools, hospitals and the courts. Discourse analysis as guide to reform seeks to expose the ways in which language is used ideologically to maintain unequal power relations in society, but it also aspires to bring about positive change in social and institutional practices.

One forum which provides a space for discourse analysis as guide to reform is the journal *Discourse and Society*, edited by Teun van Dijk. Papers published in *Discourse and Society* present analyses of talk and text which explore the relationship between discourse and power relations. Newspaper reporting, radio programmes, literature, promotional publications, institutional interviews and ordinary conversations provide material for analysis. The primary objective of the papers is to expose the ways in which discursive constructions and rhetorical strategies promote particular versions of reality and how these versions suit powerful interest groups. However, many papers do address the question of possible applications of findings in their concluding paragraphs. Even though application does not constitute the main focus of the papers, authors do acknowledge the importance of intervention and they attempt to identify appropriate strategies. Five major strategies can be identified in *Discourse and Society*:

1 *Providing a space for alternative constructions.* Here, the discourse analyst provides a space for alternative discourses to be heard. Through the selection of a particular text, the analyst actively reinforces a particular version of reality. For example, Rymes (1995) discusses the construction of moral agency in the narratives of two high school drop-outs. She suggests that her research helped to create a space for the telling of a version which is not normally heard. She would like to see her work as providing 'impetus for more talk, more chances for narrative between diverse people and to work together in the struggle to evolve moral meaning through life' (Rymes 1995: 513).

2 *Therapeutic interventions.* Discourse analysis can be used as a way of examining the construction of selves. Its therapeutic potential lies in its emphasis upon flexibility and change through the use of language. For example, O'Connor (1995) analyses the autobiographical narratives of violent criminal acts as told by inmates, with a particular focus on those utterances which break the telling frame. O'Connor proposes that the speaker's reflexive frame breaks can be a starting point for rehabilitative talk. She concludes that 'this research shows that promoting discursive interventions is one step toward helping prisoners to see themselves as agents' (O'Connor 1995: 452).

3 *Education.* Discourse analysis can also be used reflexively as a form of educational consciousness raising. Here, individuals are encouraged to examine critically how and with what consequences discourses position them and others. For example, Nilan (1995) explores the negotiation of gendered identity within the context of a collective creative writing exercise in a secondary school. Having demonstrated how the collective production of a cultural text involves the students in reflective and analytical activity, she advocates the pedagogic practice of inviting male and female students 'to consider thoughtfully not only the ideological constitution of the gendered social world, but also how the collective practices of everyday talk and behaviour activate the construction, reconstruction, and potentially also deconstruction, of their gendered social world' (Nilan 1995: 45).

4 *Campaigning.* Discourse analytic studies can inform campaigning strategies. For example, Hackett and Zhao (1994) analysed an archive of US newspaper articles covering the anti-Gulf War protests. They identified three dominant interpretive frames as well as largely defensive voices from within the peace movement. They relate these patterns of press discourse to America's master narrative of war, and conclude by spelling out the implications of their findings for future campaigning strategies of the peace movement. Hackett and Zhao recommend to the peace movement the identification of militarism as a cultural problem and 'to build coalitions which transcend purely reactive, negative politics, toward proposing a compelling alternative vision of what America could be' (Hackett and Zhao 1994: 539).

5 *Lobbying*. Discourse analyses of media presentations explore constructions and positionings of different social groups and their implications for such groups' social and personal life experience. Discourse analysts can use their findings in order to lobby policy-makers, media producers and politicians. For example, Harwood and Giles (1992) present a discourse analysis of the TV show *The Golden Girls*. They draw attention to the way in which the show perpetuates stereotypes of the elderly by presenting counter-stereotypical portrayals as laughable. They conclude by recommending that television producers seek out sources of humour other than age as well as presentations of elderly characters in genres other than comedy.

In her book *Discourses of Disorder*, Wodak (1996) explores the ways in which institutional discourses maintain and legitimate existing power relations within schools, hospitals, the media and therapy. She also attempts to use the results of her analyses in order to develop proposals which will alter the linguistic practices of people in these settings. Wodak's discussion of intervention is informed by an awareness that changes in discourse which are intended to be liberating may end up by mystifying power structures and therefore perpetuate the very inequalities they were designed to challenge. For example, her analysis of transcripts of school committee meetings in Austrian schools reveals that democratic structures were used by more powerful participants (e.g. heads, principals, chairpersons) in order to push their own agendas and achieve their preferred results. Wodak (1996: 98) concludes that 'democracy cannot be established from above . . . in a hierarchical domain . . . In this case, democratization reveals itself as a myth.' At the same time, Wodak maintains that there are domains within which (changes in) communication practices can advance the interests of those who lack power. She refers to doctor–patient communication and therapeutic discourse as positive examples. Wodak recommends that we do three things when we practice discourse analysis as guide to reform. First, we make transparent inequality and domination. Second, we propose possibilities of change. Third, we identify the limits of possible emancipation through new patterns of discourse alone (see Wodak 1996: 32).

Discourse analysis as guide to reform depends upon the willingness of policy-makers, politicians and professionals to cooperate with its recommendations. Since discourse analysis as guide to reform is committed to radical social change and to the struggle against domination, oppression and inequality, it is unlikely that those who have the power to change institutional practices would embrace recommendations based upon critical discourse analysis. Reform, as opposed to revolutionary change, must be acceptable to those whose power is grounded in the status quo. As a result, discourse analysis as guide to reform is likely to have to make compromises in order to intervene within existing social institutions.

Another problem with discourse analysis as guide to reform is its suscept-ibility to idealism. Recommendations for discursive changes tend to be levelled at professionals such as doctors, judges, teachers, journalists and so on. It is assumed that they are able to drive discursive change. However, professionals' communication practices tend to be grounded within material and social structures, such as hierarchies, physical spaces and economic constraints. For example, Wodak (1996: 61) argues that doctor–patient com-munication at a Viennese hospital was characterized by 'inefficient behaviour patterns which could be changed relatively easily, even inside the existing structures of medical institutions'. These behaviour patterns were maintained by a series of 'myths' which the medical staff subscribe to. Popular 'myths' include 'the myth of efficiency' and 'the myth of time'. Wodak argues that medical staff can, and should, relinquish these myths in order to improve patient care. However, it is likely that the 'myths' Wodak refers to do have a material basis and that it is very difficult, if not impossible, for medical staff simply to abandon them. For instance, it may be true that time is often wasted and that available time could be used more constructively; however, in order to do this, medical staff need to have the space (mental and physical) to enable them to make the required changes.

## Conclusion

The chapters in this book address the question of the applicability of dis-course analytic work. All of them acknowledge that the relationship between discourse analysis and application is problematic, but they vary in the extent to which they are prepared to make recommendations for concrete interven-tions. The chapters in this book resonate with the three discourse analytic approaches to practice outlined in this introduction; discourse analysis as social critique, discourse analysis as empowerment and discourse analysis as guide to reform. Where they do make concrete proposals for improved social practice, they discuss the specific limitations and risks associated with these particular interventions. Conversely, where there is a reluctance to apply discourse analytic research, this is acknowledged and reasons for this position are provided. All chapters follow a common structure. They introduce the social practice they are concerned with (e.g. police suspect interviewing or sex education) and critically discuss the relevance of applied psychology to this practice. This is followed by an account of the author's approach to discourse analysis (e.g. thematic deconstruction or discursive psychology) and a presentation of a discourse analysis of chosen texts (e.g. self-help books or semi-structured interviews). The chapters conclude by discussing the ways in which their discourse analysis can inform social and/or psychological interventions and by identifying any advantages and disadvantages associated with such interventions.

# References

Ajzen, I. (1988) *Attitudes, Personality and Behaviour*. Chicago, IL: Dorsey Press.

Ajzen, I. and Fishbein, M. (1980) *Understanding Attitudes and Predicting Social Behaviour*. Englewood Cliffs, NJ: Prentice Hall.

Alldred, P. (1996) Whose expertise? Conceptualizing resistance to advice about childrearing. In E. Burman, G. Aitken, P. Alldred, R. Allwood, T. Billington, B. Goldberg, A. J. Gordo Lopez, C. Heenan, D. Marks and S. Warner (eds) *Psychology, Discourse and Social Practice: From Regulation to Resistance*. London: Taylor and Francis.

Allwood, R. (1996) 'I have depression, don't I?' Discourses of help and self-help books. In E. Burman, G. Aitken, P. Alldred, R. Allwood, T. Billington, B. Goldberg, A. J. Gordo Lopez, C. Heenan, D. Marks and S. Warner (eds) *Psychology, Discourse and Social Practice: From Regulation to Resistance*. London: Taylor and Francis.

Atkinson, R. C. (1977) Reflections on psychology's past and concerns about its future, *American Psychologist*, 32(3): 205–10.

Banister, P., Burman, E., Parker, I., Taylor, M. and Tindall, C. (1994) *Qualitative Methods in Psychology: A Research Guide*. Buckingham: Open University Press.

Billig, M. (1987) *Arguing and Thinking: A Rhetorical Approach to Social Psychology*. Cambridge: Cambridge University Press.

Burman, E. (1996) Psychology discourse practice, from regulation to resistance. In E. Burman, G. Aitken, P. Alldred, R. Allwood, T. Billington, B. Goldberg, A. J. Gordo Lopez, C. Heenan, D. Marks and S. Warner (eds) *Psychology, Discourse and Social Practice: From Regulation to Resistance*. London: Taylor and Francis.

Burman, E., Aitken, G., Alldred, P., Allwood, R., Billington, T., Goldberg, B., Gordo Lopez, A. J., Heenan, C., Marks, D. and Warner, S. (eds) (1996) *Psychology, Discourse and Social Practice: From Regulation to Resistance*. London: Taylor and Francis.

Burman, E. and Parker, I. (eds) (1993) *Discourse Analytic Research: Repertoires and Readings of Texts in Action*. London: Routledge.

Burr, V. (1995) *An Introduction to Social Constructionism*. London: Routledge.

Carr, W. and Kemmis, S. (1986) *Becoming Critical: Education, Knowledge and Action Research*. London: Falmer Press.

Colman, A. (1994) Psychological evidence in South African murder trials, *The Psychologist*, 4(11): 482–6.

Crawford, J., Kippax, S., Onyx, J., Gault, U. and Benton, P. (1992) *Emotion and Gender: Constructing Meaning from Memory*. London: Sage.

Cromby, J. and Standen, P. (1996) Psychology in the service of the state, *Psychology, Politics, Resistance*, 3, Spring/Summer, 6–7.

Curt, B. C. (1994) *Textuality and Tectonics: Troubling Social and Psychological Science*. Buckingham: Open University Press.

Edwards, D. and Potter, J. (1992) *Discursive Psychology*. London: Sage.

Epston, D. and White, M. (1989) *Literate Means to Therapeutic Ends*. Adelaide: Dulwich Centre Publications.

Gergen, K. (1985) The social constructionist movement in modern psychology, *American Psychologist*, 40(3): 266–75.

Hackett, R. A. and Zhao, Y. (1994) Challenging a master narrative: peace protest and opinion/editorial discourse in the US press during the Gulf War, *Discourse and Society*, 5(4): 509–41.

Harré, R. (1986) *The Social Construction of Emotion*. Oxford: Basil Blackwell.

Hart, E. and Bond, M. (1995) *Action Research for Health and Social Care: A Guide to Practice*. Buckingham: Open University Press.

Harwood, J. and Giles, H. (1992) 'Don't make me laugh': age representations in a humorous context, *Discourse and Society*, 3(4): 403–36.

Henriques, J., Hollway, W., Urwin, C., Venn, C. and Walkerdine, V. (1984) *Changing the Subject: Psychology, Social Regulation and Subjectivity*. London: Methuen.

Hollway, W. (1989) *Subjectivity and Method in Psychology: Gender, Meaning and Science*. London: Sage.

Howitt, D. (1991) *Concerning Psychology: Psychology Applied to Social Issues*. Buckingham: Open University Press.

Kitzinger, C. and Thomas, A. (1995) Sexual harrassment: a discursive approach. In S. Wilkinson and C. Kitzinger (eds) *Feminism and Discourse: Psychological Perspectives*. London: Sage.

Levine, M. and Perkins, D. V. (1987) *Principles of Community Psychology: Perspectives and Applications*. Oxford: Oxford University Press.

Lewin, K. (1946) Action research and minority problems. In G. W. Lewin (ed.) *Resolving Social Conflicts: Selected Papers on Group Dynamics by Kurt Lewin*. New York: Harper and Brothers.

Lovering, K. M. (1995) The bleeding body: adolescents talk about menstruation. In S. Wilkinson and C. Kitzinger (eds) *Feminism and Discourse: Psychological Perspectives*. London: Sage.

Nilan, P. (1995) Negotiating gender identity in classroom disputes and collaboration, *Discourse and Society*, 6(1): 27–47.

O'Connor, P. E. (1995) Speaking of crime: 'I don't know what made me do it', *Discourse and Society*, 6(3): 429–56.

Orford, J. (1992) *Community Psychology: Theory and Practice*. Chichester: Wiley.

Parker, I. (1992) *Discourse Dynamics: Critical Analysis for Social and Individual Psychology*. London: Routledge.

Parker, I. (ed.) (1999) *Critical Textwork*. Buckingham: Open University Press.

Parker, I., Georgaca, E., Harper, D., McLaughlin, T. and Stowell-Smith, M. (1995) *Deconstructing Psychopathology*. London: Sage.

Potter, J. (1982) '. . . Nothing so practical as a good theory'. The problematic application of social psychology. In P. Stringer (ed.) *Confronting Social Issues: Some Applications of Social Psychology, Volume 1*. London: Academic Press.

Potter, J. and Wetherell, M. (1987) *Discourse and Social Psychology: Beyond Attitudes and Behaviour*. London: Sage.

Potter, J. and Wetherell, M. (1995) Discourse analysis. In J. A. Smith, R. Harré and L. Van Langenhove (eds) *Rethinking Methods in Psychology*. London: Sage.

Reicher, S. (1994) Politics of crowd psychology, *The Psychologist*, 4(11): 487–91.

Rymes, B. (1995) The construction of moral agency in the narratives of high-school drop-outs, *Discourse and Society*, 6(4): 495–516.

Sacks, H. (1992) *Lectures on Conversation, Volumes 1 and 2* (ed. G. Jefferson). Oxford: Blackwell.

Semin, G. R. and Fiedler, K. (1996) *Applied Social Psychology*. London: Sage.
Stenner, P. (1993) Discoursing jealousy. In E. Burman and I. Parker (eds) *Discourse Analytic Research: Repertoires and Readings of Texts in Action*. London: Routledge.
van Elteren, M. (1992) Karl Korsch and Lewinian social psychology: failure of a project, *History of the Human Sciences*, 5(2): 33–61.
Wetherell, M. and Potter, J. (1992) *Mapping the Language of Racism*. Hemel Hempstead: Harvester Wheatsheaf.
Widdicombe, S. (1995) Identity, politics and talk: a case for the mundane and the everyday. In S. Wilkinson and C. Kitzinger (eds) *Feminism and Discourse: Psychological Perspectives*. London: Sage.
Widdicombe, S. and Woofitt, R. (1995) *The Language of Youth Subcultures: Social Identity in Action*. Hemel Hempstead: Harvester Wheatsheaf.
Wilkinson, S. and Kitzinger, C. (1995) *Feminism and Discourse: Psychological Perspectives*. London: Sage.
Willig, C. (1997) The limitations of trust in intimate relationships: constructions of trust and sexual risk-taking, *British Journal of Social Psychology*, 36: 211–21.
Wodak, R. (1996) *Disorders of Discourse*. Harlow: Addison Wesley Longman.

# 2 Stress as regimen:
## critical readings of self-help literature

### STEVEN D. BROWN

Write a scathing letter to a relative you find it difficult to cope with, listing every resentment. But don't send it.

(Faelton and Diamond 1989: 57)

## Stress and the shaping of conduct

Somewhere in between the psychology and the health sections in your local bookseller, you will find them all neatly lined up – row upon row of books with titles like *Coping with Stress*, *Stress Relief* or *Stress Control*. There are titles aimed specifically at women, at families and at harassed executives (*60 Second Stress Management*, an oxymoron if ever there was). And for those for whom the very thought of picking up a book about stress is itself a source of anxiety, there is always Paul Wilson's pocket sized bestseller *The Little Book of Calm*. Clearly there is a demand here for something, but precisely what is a little difficult to grasp. It is worth recalling that these kinds of books are among the oldest body of literature in existence: the advice manual or written regimen, whose origins can be traced back through medieval texts on *regimen sanitatis* to Pythagoras's dire written warnings on the dangers of consuming beans. So there is nothing new in the format. Perhaps, then, there is something particularly striking in the fact that all these books are concerned with the 'stressful' effects of 'modern life' on the individual. Yet this was precisely the frame for George Beard's popular treatise on American nervousness in 1881, as well as a whole genre of books published in the UK and the USA in the first half of the twentieth century which went under such glorious titles as *Release from Nervous Tension*, *Relax and Live* and *Do Something about Those Nerves*. In many ways, 'stress' as the theme of the current books inherits many of its key motifs from this earlier concern with 'nerves'.

Here is the problem I want to explore in this chapter: what precisely is going on in and with this literature? As a social psychologist who works with discourse analysis, I believe that this kind of question is more than idle reflection on the fads and trends of the publishing industry. Let us leave aside for a moment what motivates people to buy or read a self-help book about stress. Consider instead what happens as they work through the text. Perhaps they feel they understand themselves and their lives a little better. Maybe they try out a few of the exercises which every such text contains: say, scoring a list of stressful events that have happened to them, or attempting a few relaxation techniques. In so doing, readers set about shuffling the bits and pieces of order which constitute their lives into some different patterns. Memories of prior events come to take on a new significance, that constant ache across the shoulder blades seems far more pressing, difficult relationships now take a new health-related dimension.

I find it helpful to understand this process through using a spatial metaphor. The text and its associated regimen open up a space where readers/adherents are impelled to work upon themselves. This takes the double form of a revision in how people understand and place value on the various aspects of their lives, the kinds of narratives about themselves they are prepared to author and, simultaneously, a switch in the kinds of activities and occupations in which they are prepared to engage. Note that I am not suggesting that reading *Coping with Stress* or the like necessarily alters someone's life, merely that it can serve to unfold a space where some fairly potent work of personal reconstruction can proceed. By taking up a position in such a space through the act of reading and following regimen, the person is led to put the important elements of his or her life into place in a way which is potentially very different to the prior configuration.

So in some sense what we have here is a classic psychological question about the shaping of conduct and understanding. I want, though, to hold off from making any hasty comments about how such a shaping might be determined, since the situation is more ambiguous than it might first appear. Although stress self-help texts contain a great many prescriptions, none really offers the reader a blueprint for a new life. What they contain are prompts, suggestions, encouragement. Desired states of mind and body are described in fulsome terms, certainly, but there is never a clear route offered to their achievement. Indeed, much of what is actually offered is hardly unique to the literature, being self-consciously described by many authors as 'plain common sense'. So how do these texts exert their effects? I believe that the answer lies in this dual aspect of understanding and regimen. The more readers begin to revise their grasp of their personal circumstances in terms of 'stress', so do they come to see themselves as engaged in a work of 'coping', for which they perceive themselves as being in dire need of a sufficiently robust regimen. Conversely, the more the adherents practise the exercises and set about changing their daily routines, so do they stand in need of some kind of explanation or set of narratives which will allow them to organize these activities into a coherent rationale. Text and regimen – that is, discourse and exercise – 'call out' to one another, and so come mutually to reinforce each other as they mark out the boundaries of this peculiar space of potential transformation.[1]

If this dual structuring of space is what is going on 'in' self-help literature, then what is going on 'with' these books is that they are subtly delimiting the 'correct' kinds of conduct which are appropriate for people who are prepared to understand themselves as 'stressed'. And this is what makes this body of literature so worthy of study, because the kind of public conduct which the books are actively seeking to bring about is one which we might well want to question. Take the opening quotation. Here it is suggested in all seriousness that the best way to deal with a difficult relationship is not to talk with or otherwise challenge the other in question, but instead to perform a mimicry of that approach by writing down one's feelings, yet leaving them uncommunicated. This kind of advice is very common in the literature. Another text suggests: 'Don't be afraid of using any control button you have – you can start with the "off" button for the stressful parts of late night news' (Hanson 1987: 35).

This is a most perplexing definition of 'control' as the power to retreat from distressing events, a definition that seems entirely at odds with what we would usually understand as personal empowerment. Note also that, in both examples, the exercise becomes explicable only once one has first 'bought into' the discourse about stress which the text promulgates, thereby defining relationship difficulties and watching distressing images as 'stressful'. Clearly, the ways of being promoted by such advice are, at best, conservative and apolitical. Such advice is in the broadest sense of the term 'ideological', perhaps even to the degree suggested by Crawford (1980), whereby individual health and self-responsibility (i.e. 'healthism') come to be seen as an overarching social good, or Young (1980), who holds that the very vagueness of the term 'stress' serves to mask a political economy entirely centred on the vicissitudes of the liberal-humanist subject. But the hook-up in these texts between this remarkably flexible notion of 'stress' and the extraordinary range of advice given is so variable that one is led to suspect that we will not get very far by specifying in advance the ideological leanings of the authors. It is better, I think, to explore just how 'stress' is built up in the narratives as a central explanatory principle and then carefully inserted into the exercises as rationale.

## A word about method

The form of discourse analysis that I want to use to explore stress self-help literature is a mixed approach which contains elements of the rhetorical analysis suggested by Billig *et al.* (1988) and the concern with metaphor as found in Potter and Wetherell (1987), and draws upon the thematic decomposition developed by Stenner (1993) and Curt (1994). The reason for settling upon this mixed method is that as an object of study the literature constitutes an uneven corpus. Although all the books analysed are about 'stress', they approach that topic from a bewildering variety of directions. Some are texts written by medical practitioners, eager to promote 'healthy living'; others are by academics keen to show how what they define as scientific knowledge can be applied to 'everyday life'; others still are by herbalists, physiotherapists, osteopaths and broadcasters. Thus what the reader stands to gain through understanding how to cope with 'stress' is described very differently by each author. For Dore, 'Understanding more about stress and how to handle it helps us to learn to make positive decisions and choices, and lead fuller, more rewarding lives as a result' (Dore 1990: 6). The appeal here is to better lives brought about through making informed life choices. Contrast this with a more hard-nosed pitch from Klarreich:

> Although, in recent years, many books have been written on the subject, more employees than ever before are suffering from stress and burnout. Why? First, because many of the books are not relevant to the workplace, and second, most of these books teach people to avoid or become distracted from their problems, rather than to deal with them directly. What is needed is a realistic and practical approach which gets at the root of these problems.
>
> (Klarreich 1988: v)

This is the language of practical measures and increased personal efficacy, with no time for idle worrying over 'positive choices' here. Finally, there are the desperate circumstances outlined by Coleman:

> Staying alive and healthy today is like staying alive and healthy in the middle of a war. The ever-present enemy is not armed with tanks or machine guns, and kills and maims not with bullets but with stress. Before you can defend yourself you need information about the enemy.
>
> (Coleman 1978: Preface)

On this account, knowing about stress is literally a matter of life or death. The reader can only survive by becoming informed. What needs to be analysed, then, is how these three diverse objectives can all converge on the same term through a range of rhetorical moves (involving metaphor, shared themes or narratives).

As soon as one starts to consider the kind of rhetorical work that goes on in these texts, one is immediately struck by both the consistency with which a common number of narratives recur and the sheer variety of the sorts of themes and rhetorical commonplaces which each text weaves around these narratives. Thus, my aim here is to try to flesh out something of the relations between narrative and other discursive devices, while retaining their apparent 'messiness'. This 'mess' is itself interesting, since it consists of fragments of Western science, holistic medicine, Eastern religion and neo-conservative economics, all of which are assembled together into intricate rhetorical patterns. The word I have found most useful to describe this discursive bricolage is 'textuality' (see Brown 1996, 1997; see also Curt 1994; Stenner and Eccleston 1994).

The following sections are organized into three tranches, based around analysis of 22 self-help texts.[2] In the first I describe the common narratives found across the corpus, and outline how they combine to draw the reader towards regimen. The second then unpacks some of the metaphors which are interleaved with these narratives, and notes some of the prescriptions they warrant. In the last tranch I discuss the representation of the psychological subject which can be reconstructed from the texts, and then try to situate this within a shared concern around 'energy'. To conclude, I make some suggestions about how this kind of analysis can be usefully applied.

## Narratives

The following narratives are assembled by way of a thematic reading of the texts. This reading is focused by concentrating on the points in each text where stress is mobilized as a framing device that constructs the 'problem' for the reader that the suggested regimen will then address. In the present corpus of texts, five narratives are used with some regularity to achieve such a framing. The names I have assigned each narrative are purely descriptive (in the texts themselves the narrative status of each framing is never acknowledged).

### The twentieth-century disease

This narrative concentrates on impressing and encouraging concern over the widespread nature of stress as a factor in ill health through the rhetorical deployment of unsubstantiated facts and figures: 'in an average lifetime the average employee loses one and a half years from work because of a stress-induced illness' (Coleman 1988: 9). This is presented as a unique and unprecedented situation. Only recently, it is claimed, has stress been recognized by advanced bio-medicine as the late 'twentieth-century plague' (Looker and Gregson 1989: 6). It is held as a matter of urgency that stress be treated as the major 'epidemic' (Lawson 1978) or 'virus' (Thompson 1982) present at the close of the century, in much the same way that tuberculosis or influenza marked its beginning:

> It is becoming obvious that not only may we suffer from the impact of stress on our lives, but many of us may actually die of disorders which are related to our inability to cope successfully with it. In an age when medical science has all but conquered life-threatening diseases, we find ourselves faced with the prospect of suffering, and possibly dying, from diseases which, although perhaps not all wholly caused by stress, have stress as a significant contributor.
>
> (Patel 1992: 7)

Stress touches upon every aspect of our lives, such that it is almost a global condition, 'our civilization's sickness' (Thompson 1982: 10). There is no social role or way of living in the contemporary world which does not contain a measure of suffering. Simply no one finds it possible to live a stress-free life:

> the young mother may suffer from feelings of inadequacy in meeting the variety of demands made on her by her children . . . The factory worker . . . may suffer acutely from the stress derived from the sheer repetitive monotony of the production line . . . The teacher will have to cope with day-to-day stress in the classroom, intensified by discipline problems and inadequate resources.
>
> (Dore 1990: 12)

The overall achievement of the narrative is to effect a generalized transformation of practically all kinds of social hardship and dis-ease into the phenomenon of stress. This constitutes a vital step in delineating an inclusive problem to be addressed by the solution of regimen.

## The primitive response syndrome

The focus of this narrative is on explaining the relation between stress and the human body. The origins of the biological and behavioural responses that are made to stress are nearly always held to be archaic. They are described as 'inherent in the human condition' (Consumers' Association 1992: 9), thereby constituting an integral part of our evolutionary heritage. It is possible to trace the formation of these longstanding human stress responses to the demands placed upon our earliest recognizable ancestors: 'prehistoric man must have found the ever present danger of man eating animals threatening and stressful' (Trauer 1986: 12).

From this the 'fight or flight' response developed. The human response to threatening stimuli (i.e. man-eating animals) was either aggressive confrontation or rapid fleeing. This is the basis upon which strategies of survival are formulated. We maintain this original tendency to the current day, with the obvious exception that the threats in current existence are of a very different nature to those faced by the early humans. This creates a unique difficulty:

> The queue at the supermarket checkout and the traffic jam can become the fangs of the sabre-toothed tiger and when confronted by these threats we respond just as if that tiger were there – by activating our caveman stress response. Having activated our body for an immediate physical response, there is often no need or opportunity for physical action! . . . We cannot fight the queue; we cannot run away from it either. So we become impatient and irritated; we become angry; we fume!
> (Looker and Gregson 1989: 26)

The current scourge of stress disease is related to this mismatch between the shape of the modern world and in-built human capacities to cope with it. Use of this narrative gives the appearance of an evolutionary dimension to the problem.

### The fast pace of modern life

The shape of the 'modern world' is the subject of extended consideration in another narrative form. The rapid developments of the past hundred years (i.e. 'progress') are contrasted with the leisurely pace of previous social organization. The current epoch is lived at breakneck speed, reflected in: 'major changes in life at all levels, from the invention of the motor car to the appearance of the test tube baby' (Dore 1990: 8). This fast progression does not obey the logic of natural variation and diversity, but represents a different, chaotic way of advancing led by industrial manufacturing and modern technology: 'So we have achieved a dizzying rate of change, not by an orderly process of biological evolution, but by the frenzied maelstrom of technological revolution' (Norfolk 1979: 38).

Technological advances usher in a new range of stresses, 'many of them psychological or social in nature' (Consumers' Association 1992: 9). These include the dissolution of the extended family and the alienating conditions of modern industrial and executive labour (Norfolk 1979). Modern stress is constructed as qualitatively different from 'primitive' or 'natural' stress. Our ancestors, the narrative concludes, were born into a world that was by its very nature dangerous and stressful. We moderns, by contrast, make our worlds stressful through our misplaced commitment to 'progress', a mistake that is now historically irreversible.

## Seeing things differently

It should not be assumed that everyone will experience stress in the same way, or even find the same things stressful in the first place. This particular narration of what stress is places weight upon the role played by individual evaluation:

> Everyone of us experiences a good amount of stress almost every day. Some of us seem to take it in their stride, while others are over-whelmed. What accounts for the difference? . . . The answer lies in the way we perceive a situation. Given the same set of circumstances, one person may see a crisis where another finds an invigorating challenge.
> (Faelton and Diamond 1989: 6)

Differences in how the world is 'seen' can result in opposing sets of feelings, either of frustration and anxiety or of challenge and stimulation. This in turn depends on the kind of 'mental attitude' or 'belief' (Dore 1990) that one brings to the situation. This also holds for the opposing situation, when one requires not a release from stress, but a measure of stimulation to inject interest into life:

> Housewives bored by the endless repetition of routine household chores will perk themselves up by investing in a new hair style; apathetic schoolchildren will raise their adrenaline levels by performing elabor-ate dares; middle-aged businessmen will break the monotony of their humdrum office lives by waging a brief, but nevertheless stimulating, affair with a young coquette from the typing pool.
> (Norfolk 1979: 35–6)

Here some moderation is introduced into the problem of stress, by indicat-ing that there is a role for the subjective. This opens out the possibility that there may be room for personal change.

## Juggling work and home

Changing roles are incorporated as a further aspect of stress. Women and men are represented as varying greatly in the kinds of things that they find stressful: 'Job stress, or lack of a job, is clearly identified as one of the major causes for men drinking; women are more likely to turn to drink because of stress in relationships' (Consumers' Association 1992: 29). This difference – reported as plain biological fact – follows through into the relative efficacy of 'coping': 'Perhaps this is why women are often so much more adaptable than men; they have to adjust to the changing physical and emotional symptoms of the menstrual cycle so they have plenty of practice' (Madders 1988: 101).

Differences are also considered in terms of the division of home and work. Stress tends to be ameliorated when a balance can be struck between the major aspects of a person's life: 'a happy home life with few major worries can help us ride through the pressures of work without distress' (Looker and Gregson 1989: 24). This is described as an escalating problem for women who juggle responsibilities in managing the family activities between home, office and school (Faelton and Diamond 1989). Part of the assumption of differences between sexes is that women are described as traditionally involved with the 'emotional' environment of the home, rather than the 'rational' environment of the workplace. Increasing movement towards the latter results in a qualitatively different set of stressors:

> Women in the past tended to be insulated from the battlefield, from cigarettes . . . and from the hurry sickness of assembly line by their role in society. Pressures of child raising . . . are not to be minimised as a source of stress. However, they have generally not involved constant conflict with the time clock.
>
> (Hanson 1987: 28)

This change is indicative of an overall uncertainty over roles in the modern world. Stress arises in both the 'dual career marriage' and 'role strain' at work (Dore 1990). What may be required is a form of domestic planning every bit as rigorous as industrial time management (Faelton and Diamond 1989). Failure at this task may be disastrous, since poor parenting is a factor in the further transmission of stress to children: 'And there we have the potential neurotic of the future, because she has been raised in an atmosphere of stress and strain, unexpressed fear and insecurity, uncertainties, and often disharmony' (Lawson 1978: 36).

This narrative manages to combine biological reductionism with commonplace observation about changes in the workplace. The effect is to present the issue of women and child care as subsumed to that of 'social stress' in general.

## Summary

Taken together, these five narratives compose the major ways in which the 'problem' of stress is constructed, to which self-help texts provide 'the answer'. As is the case with most forms of regimen, the solution is not posed as law, but as a choice which is available to the person: 'You have a choice in life . . . You can be stressed, you can be burned out, or you can be reasonably happy and productive and enjoy a meaningful career' (Klarreich 1988: 160). Being 'burned out' is here a matter of choice because the solution offered by regimen exists, and has been offered up to the reader, who presumably now understands the inescapable condition of stress that otherwise awaits them. A grand gesture of extending wisdom and guidance is played out. The reader must further accept the serious nature of the choice he or she is making, and that it involves assuming an active role: 'This is not a book for hypochondriacs. It is for people who enjoy being healthy and are prepared to help themselves to remain healthy' (Eagle 1982: 6). The work of staying healthy is purely a matter of personal responsibility. The texts offer help, but on the proviso that readers fully accept that the problem lies within themselves (and not within the structure of the world around them). Change is only possible if individuals are able to 'own' (Powell 1993) their distress: 'the fact that stress is mostly an experience that we create for ourselves means that only we as individuals can control and manage our own stress' (Looker and Gregson 1989: 7).

Having established the conditions under which one must assume regimen, the texts offer numerous descriptions of the road which must be followed. It may be that of modifying our current ways of thinking through a policy of 'developing the right mental attitudes' (Dore 1990: 15). The tasks may involve 'counter-thinking' (Klarreich 1988), or a commitment to 'reflective coping' (Faelton and Diamond 1989). The eventual state which the initiate may hope to achieve through his or her labours is that of becoming 'stresswise' (Looker and Gregson 1989), 'stress resistant' (Hanson 1987) or 'stress inoculated' (Meichenbaum 1983).

## Devices

Although narrative acts to frame the space within which the followers of regimen will (supposedly) transform their life, the major features of that space are marked out by the use of a number of rhetorical devices. These consist of metaphors, tropes and rhetorical commonplaces which allow readers to think through their relationship to their body and to 'stress' in ways which are oriented towards a particular type of practical activity. Such devices regularly occur before a particular piece of advice is given (often formulated analogically, in the manner of 'think of it like this . . .' or 'your body is like . . .'). This positioning means that the device comes to serve as the formal grounds upon which the often bizarre advice subsequently suggested comes to appear perfectly rational and efficacious. A selection of the major devices sampled from the present corpus of books follows.

### Heat

Some rhetorical devices function by reducing the qualities of whatever entities they are used to describe into one simple action-attribute.[3] In stress self-help texts the notion of 'heat' works in this way. Its application reduces description into a movement from cooler/hotter. For example, one text advises that during a traffic jam drivers should 'keep themselves and their car cool' (Consumers' Association 1992: 69). By aligning the overheating car with the state of the human body, the device 'explains' by analogy what is occurring in the situation. This brings with it a range of implications for action: overheating results in loss of function and possible damage, but it can be avoided by taking measures to restore coolness. The use of devices such as 'heat' serves to make stress visible in a way that is immediately explicable to the reader. In so doing it solves the problem of how to make an otherwise vague scientific concept literally shine forth from the human body. The character of a 'type A' person can, for example, be grasped straight away when he or she is referred to as a 'hot reactor' (Faelton and Diamond 1989). In another text, a cartoon of a 'stressed person' is drawn with his head tapering into an exploding volcano, spewing forth the words 'rage' and 'roars' (Meichenbaum 1983: 126). Visual juxtaposition of this kind conceals the analogical nature of the device (there is actually no straight-forward correlation between human body temperature and 'stress'). This is most apparent when heat is used as shorthand for the entire experience of being stressed, as in the condition 'burnout'. Explaining the proper treatment for 'burnout' becomes a simple matter of working through the hotter/cooler function: 'stopping the burning, reducing the heat, getting out of the fire and making the heat bearable' (Powell 1993: 40).

There is a great deal of rhetorical work compressed here. It implies that stress involves some form of 'burning' occurring to the body, produced by the 'fire' of the environment, from which the afflicted person may 'leap to safety'. The work is not obvious, however, because of the taken-for-granted character of associated cultural commonplaces, such as getting out when one cannot 'stand the heat in the kitchen' (Faelton and Diamond 1989: 50). Heat may also be embedded as the organizing principle for more complex analogies, such as a description of the body as constructed like a central heating system (De Vries 1985: 56). The hotter/cooler function is here wedded to an engineering analogy to present a general picture of the composition of the body itself and its different states (i.e. running efficiently or not, the power of the main pump and so on). In either case, the rhetorical potency of the analogy makes the device extremely difficult to refuse (who would not at least be tempted by the proposition that one's 'stress' could be fixed as speedily as a leaking radiator?).

## War

In a series of tropes repeated in self-help texts, the experience of stress is described as a 'battle' or 'war'. This acts as a figurative core around which more specific descriptions and narrative characters can be hung.

Most importantly, it sets in place a metaphorical relationship between self and other(s) as enemies ranged against one another in combat. The war itself is initiated by the 'forces of stress [which] are ready and able to attack you' (Silva and Goldman 1988: 67). The challenge is to 'defuse stress' (Dore 1990), by deploying 'many powerful and intricate weapons . . . in response to the "enemy"' (Hanson 1985: 37). Chief among these is the exercise of constant surveillance, since 'it is only by being aware of your stresses that you can cope with them – you cannot fight an unseen enemy' (Hanson 1985: 59). The ultimate goal is securing 'freedom from stress' (Lawson 1978) and so becoming a 'stress survivor' (Cooper and Davidson 1991).

Thus does the body of the stressed individual become a nation state unto itself, with all the moral trappings and banal justifications that entails. The active stress-resistor is a noble figure, defending territory and liberty, affirming his or her rights and way of life by taking arms against the aggressor. The resistor is impelled to struggle to the utmost, chastened by the fearful spectacle of defeat – for when 'resistance fails . . . the body surrenders' (Thompson 1982: 53). At the same time, difficulties with stress can be glossed as minor tactical errors. The best defence is sometimes, after all, to 'sound the retreat' and 'step back from the fray occasionally in order to regroup our forces and prepare for the next advance' (Norfolk 1979: 139).

Close to the core of this metaphor of stress-as-war is the utopian notion of a 'safe place' (e.g. Madders 1988; Faelton and Diamond 1989; Dore 1990). There is always somewhere to which we may retire, a 'security zone' (Norfolk 1979) where stress may not extend. But this fantasy of safety is grounded heavily in the realism of modern urban society, with its gated communities and constant surveillance. The key to resisting stress is, on this account, knowing 'how to build your defences into a virtual fortress' (Hanson 1985: 215). Indeed, precisely this kind of rhetoric is found in some of the biological sciences (in particular immunology) upon which the self-help texts loosely draw. There the metaphor of 'the body at war' (Dwyer 1988) has become absolutely entangled with a functional grasp of what the immune system does. The origins of this device may, then, be as much scientific as sociological.

## Engineering and computation

Probably the most important series of devices present in the corpus are metaphors based around engineering and computation. They are often used to explain to the reader the physiological aspects of the human stress response. This is made akin to the strain induced in iron bars (Thompson 1982), the compressing of springs (Lawson 1978) or the battering of an aeroplane in a storm (Blythe 1974). Visual depictions are often used in support, such as an image of a wooden plank splintering under increasing weight (Trauer 1986: 8). What is achieved is a sense that stress is a natural phenomenon whose laws can be directly intuited from empirical observation. Indeed, one finds much the same reliance on engineering metaphors in the early scientific literature on stress (Hinkle 1973).

Computational metaphors are deployed to a slightly different end. They impress on the reader the importance of understanding mental operations during stress as though they were predominately matters of information processing:

> Our senses pick up information about our environment and pass this to the brain for processing, interpretation and decision making . . . Once the brain has decided on a course of action, the 'get set' instructions are passed to body organs to deal with the situation. It may be that the decision . . . is appropriate and our response is successful in dealing with demands. In this case we will feel no distress.
>
> (Looker and Gregson 1989: 44–5)

In one sense all this does is simply to induct the reader into the cognitive orthodoxy that dominates much contemporary psychology. But what it further buttresses is the notion that subjectivism is at the root of all human stress reactions. This peels away the social context, leaving the 'inner processes' of the individual as the sole focus: 'stress is not in the environment but is a state within you' (Looker and Gregson 1989: 40). The environment itself is reduced to a series of information flows passing through the 'mental computer' (Norfolk 1979), which handles inputs to the body in the manner of a 'fully integrated system'. The problem that arises is knowing precisely what should be counted as an appropriate response to the situation, given the lack of any clear perceptual hook-up to the wider environmental context.

This issue of veridicality is circumvented by treating stress management as an information processing problem. Much of the work needed to deal with stress can be done 'within' the individual. The texts point to natural healing processes such as 'dreaming . . . the body's way of sorting out information and problems' (Looker and Gregson 1989: 176–7) or else of 'disconnecting' for a time from the outside world during relaxation (Madders 1988). One may also learn to tackle problems consciously by doing 'an instant replay' (Faelton and Diamond 1989) or discovering how to 'programme yourself for success' (Powell 1993: 131). At a deeper level it is also possible to uncover and remove 'old parental messages in your head' (Powell 1993: 164), which are described as the real source of unwanted behaviours. The net effect of all these metaphorical transformations is to render regimen as a form of mental engineering, rather than as an aesthetic or moral activity.

## The serviceable self

When a regimen is presented to the reader as a purely technical activity, it follows that the self which will result from adhering to the prescribed exercises is to be understood as literally a 'product'. This suggests that selfhood can be 'serviced' and 're-engineered' according to the demands of lifestyle.[4] If regimen in the classical sense is the 'art of making oneself', or in more recent humanistic guises 'realizing one's full potential', then the kind of programme suggested in the present texts resembles more the purchasing of an 'upgrade' for self, or at least the 'adding on' of some new capabilities.

The image of the psychological subject as a 'serviceable self' emerges in the course of descriptions of precisely how a regimen ameliorates the effects of stress. Let us assume that stress acts as an 'accelerator' which may force the body into 'overdrive' (Klarreich 1988) and thereby disturb its 'fine tuning' (Thompson 1982). Ill health is then to be understood as a malfunction or 'mechanical breakdown' (Madders 1988) in the body, akin to a 'blown fuse' (De Vries 1985). In order to recover, it is necessary to 'switch off the stress system and switch on the relaxation system' (Consumers' Association 1992: 152). Fortuitously, the body is equipped with a 'self-curing system' (Consumers' Association 1992) which allows it to 'recharge its batteries' (Looker and Gregson 1989) over time. Careful prevention, though, will prevent the damage in the first place and ensure maximum performance:

> Just as a car can be serviced and tuned for peak performance and to avoid or reduce problems and breakdowns, so too can our bodies be prepared to run smoothly and perform well. Such self-servicing includes learning the skills to deal with stress.
>
> (Looker and Gregson 1989: 23)

The 'serviceable self' described here is one which requires regular maintenance to perform at maximum efficiency, but one which is also capable of a wide range of activities. The key trope is 'flexibility'. The person is encouraged to develop a 'flexible attitude' (Consumers' Association 1992) in all that they do. This stance allows one to decide when to persist at a particular task, when to switch tactics and when to give up (Powell 1993). Flexibility comes to take on the status of a superordinate value: 'You aim to play it safe. But today's uncertain world presents little safety. The key is to realize that the only security is within yourself . . . It also helps to be flexible' (Powell 1993: 149). To put it crudely, the message here is that one can only survive by engineering a version of oneself that is sufficiently robust and flexible to withstand the manifold and varied demands of modern life. This helpful advice owes not a little to current discourses around sociobiology and neo-classical economics (see Cot 1987; Rabinow 1992).

It also, as Emily Martin (1994) describes, chimes with the image of the 'flexible manager' found in some of the more aggressive forms of management training. Now if this were the only input into the notion of a serviceable self, then it would be easy to dismiss this vision of personal development as purely ideological. But there is another aspect to this representation of self which derives from an entirely different discourse. A disproportionate amount of material in each text is dedicated to issues surrounding 'time management'. The need to plan one's activities and tightly govern the amount of time allotted to each is often warranted by statements like this: 'Life is short. You are wasting your time, your energies and yourself in something that is destroying you' (Powell 1993: 51).

It is worth dwelling on this claim. It states that human life is irreversible, following an inexorable and all-too-brief course towards death. One is given a small measure of time and energy, and with it the responsibility to expend that time in the best possible fashion. To 'waste' such resources by allowing oneself to be stressed is merely to hasten one's ultimate demise. It is a form of suicide. Note that the implication is that it is actually impossible to avoid stress entirely: 'we would virtually have to stop living to avoid stress' (Klarreich 1988: 19). Life is inherently stressful. Or put even more succinctly, 'death is clearly the ultimate form of relaxation' (Eagle 1982: 61). People who properly understand their own stress are therefore involved in a struggle to prevent the rate at which they are 'worn down' by life. Stress management here appears as the management of a living death.

This introduces into the texts something akin to an economics of energy. While one is alive, one should attempt to stave off the inevitable by spending one's energy wisely. It may be 'conserved' by accepting what one cannot change (Lawson 1978) or through wise planning (Faelton and Diamond 1989); it may be 'invested' (Powell 1993), perhaps 'optimized' (Thompson 1982) and, of course, 'wasted' (Consumers' Association 1992). People are directed carefully to 'maximize their natural resources' (Looker and Gregson 1989: 8) by ensuring that energy is not only released properly but also directed towards the correct activity (Madders 1988). One must learn to conserve and spend the birthright wisely: 'If you husband your energy, as you would with a regular habit of relaxation, you can channel that reserved energy into your particular aims and ambitions' (Lawson 1978: 93).

There seem to be two distinct discourses mixed together in this focus on energy. The first is an understanding of energy as capital, with concomitant concerns with management of utility, investment returns and so on. This is the source of the tropes of flexibility and servicing. They all derive from a Western technical-scientific model of natural resources that reached its full ferment in the nineteenth century with the popularization of thermodynamics, not only as the science of Industrial Revolution, but also as a means to understand social organization more generally as a matter of harnessing, distributing and deploying natural labour power (see Rabinbach

1990). Combined with this is an Eastern model of the harmonious balance between forces, where 'energy' (in the sense of natural resource) is made crudely synonymous with both Chi and 'vital force' (e.g. Blythe 1973). The references to 'relaxation' and 'insight' then draw upon this understanding of personal empowerment as a matter of balancing oppositions that exist throughout nature. Thus 'management' becomes blurred with 'self-control', just as 'allocation' slides into 'balance'.

The crucial point I want to make here is that it is the very vacuousness of the terms stress and energy which makes the mixing up of these discourses possible.[5] They make it possible to unite otherwise seemingly incommensurate ways of understanding the relation of humans to the natural world, to produce a hybrid language of personal empowerment that can be extended by paralogy into a vast number of opposing directions by management consultants, herbalists and counsellors. Here is a way of speaking that really can be 'all things to all people'. But – and this is equally crucial – because stress is indissociable in the West from a technical-rational grasp of regimen as the means by which self can be 'improved' and 'serviced', the overall effect of combining the two is to produce a series of values which are structured in accord with what Thrift (1997) calls 'soft capitalism': that is, a market-driven grasp of the socio-economic order as a non-zero game played by successful entrepreneurial selves who grasp the complexities of the world by way of a taste for hastily packaged metaphysics.

## Applications . . .

Can you begin to see what is happening? You are becoming your own counsellor. You are beginning to challenge your thinking as it has never been challenged before. You are overturning the reasoning that caused your stress.

(Klarreich 1988: 74)

Self-help texts encourage readers to develop a particular relationship with themselves, one based around the notion of a desired self as product to be engineered. Such engineering can only proceed on the basis of adequate self-knowledge. Understanding stress, they assert, is the key to this knowledge. In one sense, popular books about stress merely add to all the other practices of self-making, ranging from counselling and television talk shows through to a myriad of multimedia personal development programmes, all of which envisage something like a self-as-entrepreneur to be the desired state of being (see Rose 1989, 1996; White 1992; du Gay 1996). Yet there is something different about the stress books. Nowhere else does one encounter such a range of authors and projects (not least due to the fact that they are marketed as both business and health texts), no other discourse comes quite as close as that around stress to authorizing its statements with hard science. Understanding stress – that is, being able to talk confidently in the language of self-help texts – gives one an ability to make bold, programmatic statements about how to live a 'happier, healthier, more rewarding life'.

Now, given the many problems with the kinds of advice proffered by such texts, one would not want this discourse to go entirely unchecked. The first application I want to suggest, then, is that the critical readings here can serve as a resource for understanding the work of personal transformation made possible by stress self-help texts. In my own research, I have spent a great deal of time talking to people about stress. It is not always easy in such discussions to pinpoint what precisely is at issue when the word 'stress' is invoked. When personal distress is translated into the language of stress, when someone becomes adept at authoring stories about his or her life that are framed using some of the common narratives and devices found in self-help texts, then his or her own personal concerns are necessarily reconstructed accordingly. Thus, an understanding of the materials used in this work makes it possible to disentangle the complaints, protests, excuses and anger that are entangled within it. I would suggest that one important site where this might be applied is at the greatly expanding interface between complementary medicine and the workplace. Here distressed workers are encouraged to reframe their concerns about their working lives and their health in terms of just the kind of hybrid discourse of stress and energy described previously. Clearly we need to understand just how this transformation then plays out when it becomes an accepted feature of labour relations.

At the same time, 'stress' enters into managerial discourse. Strategy documents, internal quality assessment, marketing reports – all of these can contain phrases and formulations which have their roots in self-help texts. As a related application, I suggest that the readings presented here be used as the basis for decoding the language of these business documents. One might look, for example, to see whether phrases such as 'flexibility', 'energy' or 'stress', or tropes such as 'heat', 'war' or 'computation', are repeated, either in the form of diagnoses or as desired goals for the organization. It would then be possible to follow precisely how ideas of re-engineering are used to represent the organization to itself, to explore how disputes and issues are translated into the prescriptive language of balance and maximizing resources, and subsequently to contest this move by exposing some of the contradictions that this language involves (e.g. 'energy' is not the same as 'resource', 'stress' is not equivalent to an 'imbalance of forces') or else to generate alternative metaphors which can be turned towards very different prescriptions (e.g. instead of treating stress management as a 'battle', thus reifying individualism, it might be described as an exercise in 'building community', with implications of mutual support and continuity).

Stress is also used, both in organizations and elsewhere, as a device to explain interpersonal conflict and the distress it creates. As we have seen, the tendency in much self-help discourse is to address this issue as a matter of personal empowerment, which is in turn based on a number of narratives about modern life and human biology. Rarely, though, are these narratives fully explicated. Thus another application of the critical readings is to have on record, so to speak, the full contents of each narrative such that they can stand as resources for those who may find it strategically useful to undermine accounts framed by way of such stories. For example, the 'fast pace of modern life' is often used as a rhetorical commonplace to justify the distress caused by certain work practices (e.g. systematic overwork, chronic job insecurity) on the grounds that they simply reflect the state of the modern society we dwell within. Knowing that this narrative is at least two hundred years old takes away at least some of its rhetorical power. Equally, pushing the 'seeing things differently' narrative to its *reductio ad absurdum*, by claiming that it logically implies the impossibility of any grounds for formal agreement, or, indeed, communication at all, serves to undermine the warranting function of that story.

Taking a slightly different approach, one might equally apply the material here in an exercise in debunking some of the scientific rhetoric that is used to warrant policy decisions and judicial rulings framed in terms of stress. The concept has in the past appeared as a decisive factor in industrial disputes, in debates around educational policy and within claims to medical malpractice (see Rosch 1995; Brown 1996). In order to make some kind of intervention in these kinds of circumstances, it is essential to have some means of decoupling prescriptive statements from the scientific 'facts' which are used to warrant them. In particular, it is important to know that there is no generally agreed single measure of stress, that 'facts' like the existence of the flight/fight reaction as the essence of stress are, at best, equivocal and that the kinds of scales of distressing life events which are so routinely touted in self-help texts are based on data and methods (Holmes and Rahe 1967) now greatly discredited. But it is also vital to be alerted to the kinds of tropes which are routinely deployed to suggest a basis in hard science. The presence of a reference to heat, war, engineering or computation should serve as immediate warning that whatever follows is likely to be only very loosely coupled to adequate scientific evidence.

Finally, the readings presented here could serve as the basis to construct very different popular texts about stress. One can imagine a series of alternative narratives to those already in circulation. Perhaps some which emphasize the effects of pollution and environmental abuse instead of 'the fast pace of modern life'; maybe others concerned with the historical neglect of adequate child-care provision, rather than 'juggling home and work'. In place of the devices such as 'war' and 'engineering' could stand a whole series of tropes grounded in 'civic debate' and 'care for self and other'. And in the hybrid of Western neo-classical economics and Eastern spirituality, the latter could certainly be more fully engaged with, hopefully to the occlusion of the former. If stress can support aromatherapists and personnel managers, it can certainly be deployed by all manner of other practitioners and activists.

### . . . And concerns

Of which I have a good few. Chief among them is the idea that discourse analysis could be presented as some kind of alternative to science. It is not. The critical readings here are about how scientific fact is represented and used to buttress regimen. Elsewhere (Brown 1997) I use similar methods to understand, following Latour (1987) and others, how science itself constructs facts through the technical control of representation, but nowhere do I suggest that there is fundamentally a single 'better' alternative to the scientific approach to understanding distress. Discourse analysis allows us to explore the complexities of how a techno-scientific culture distributes knowledge (always, it seems, unfairly). On a similar note, I am not trying to come to some kind of moral judgement about stress self-help texts. Not only do I doubt very much that there is any uncontested moral ground to be taken here, but I also think this misses the key point about how these books are used. Readers do what they will with them. Certainly there are tendencies, general directions in which they will be led (notably rampant apolitical individualism), but no clear overall goal. Here the value of discourse analysis is that it can reveal much of the 'mess' present in a text and draw out some of the possible threads. I make no apologies for the mixed method I have used in this chapter. My sole justification is that it seemed to fit with the data. By 'fit' I mean that it allowed me to see aspects of the texts that were previously obscured. Many other variants on discourse analysis could conceivably have been used. Were my materials snippets of conversations, or institutional vision statements and policy documents, I would have used a slightly different method. Choice of method should be informed by the quality of the results, how well they serve to inform us about the issue in question, what kind of work they make visible. Methodological purity and the demand for replication are simply not a concern when the materials under study are cultural practices. Perhaps what is a concern is how the analyst positions herself or himself in all of this. Maybe you have been waiting for me – finally – to state my relationship to these texts, what I feel is their true value. All that I can say with any absolute, complete sense of conviction is that if you choose to write a scathing letter to a relative who is difficult to cope with, then don't hesitate for a second: send the letter.

## Notes

1 This embedding of discourse and practical exercise to serve rhetorical purposes is an ancient device. It is analysed in some detail by Foucault (1979, 1986).
2 All the texts considered (listed in the references) are about either stress or a close synonym such as 'burnout'.
3 Elsewhere (Brown 1996) I have called these devices 'operators'.
4 This analysis is partly informed by Wendy Stainton Roger's (1991) exposition of 'the body as machine' account of health.
5 By this I mean that despite attempts to formulate each term scientifically, they carry a whole range of cultural values and possible interpretations – often quite deep rooted and historically intractable – that may be only loosely coupled to technical definitions.

## References

Beard, G. (1881) *American Nervousness: Its Causes and Consequences*. New York: Putnam's.
Billig, M. (1996) *Arguing and Thinking*, 2nd edn. Cambridge: Cambridge University Press.
Billig, M., Condor, S., Edwards, D., Gane, M., Middleton, D. and Radley, A. (1988) *Ideological Dilemmas*. London: Sage.
Blythe, P. (1973) *Stress Disease: The Growing Plague*. London: Arthur Baker.
Brown, S. D. (1996) The textuality of stress: drawing between scientific and every-day accounting, *Journal of Health Psychology*, 1(2): 173–93.
Brown, S. D. (1997) The life of stress: seeing and saying dysphoria, unpublished PhD thesis, University of Reading.
Coleman, V. (1978) *Stress Control: How to Cope with Anxiety*. London: Pan.
Coleman, V. (1988) *Stress Management Techniques: Managing People for Healthy Profits*. London: Mercury.
Consumers' Association (1992) *Understanding Stress*. London: Hodder & Stoughton.
Cooper, C. L. and Davidson, M. J. (1991) *The Stress Survivors: Experiences of Successful Personalities*. London: Grafton.
Cot, A. (1987) Neoconservative economics, utopia and crisis, *Zone*, 1/2: 293–311.
Crawford, R. (1980) Healthism and the medicalization of everyday life, *International Journal of Health Services*, 10: 365–88.
Curt, B. C. (1994) *Textuality and Tectonics: Troubling Social and Psychological Science*. Buckingham: Open University Press.
De Vries, J. (1985) *Stress and Nervous Disorders*. Edinburgh: Mainstream.
Dore, H. (1990) *Coping with Stress*. London: Hamlyn.
du Gay, P. (1996) *Consumption and Identity at Work*. London: Sage.
Dwyer, J. (1988) *The Body at War*. London: Unwin Hyman.
Eagle, R. (1982) *Taking the Strain*. London: British Broadcasting Corporation.
Faelton, S. and Diamond, D. (1989) *Stress Relief: An Easy-access Guide to Coping with and Avoiding Stress*. London: Ebury Press.

Fink, D. H. (1945) *Release From Nervous Tension*. London: George Allen and Unwin.

Foucault, M. (1979) My body, this paper, this fire, *Oxford Literary Review*, 4(1): 9–28.

Foucault, M. (1986) *The Care of the Self: The History of Sexuality, Volume 3*. Harmondsworth: Penguin.

Goliszek, A. (1993) *60 Second Stress Management: The Quickest Way to Relax and Ease Anxiety*. London: Bantam.

Hanson, P. (1985) *The Joy of Stress*. London: Pan.

Hinkle, L. E. (1973) The concept of stress in the biological and social sciences, *Science, Medicine and Man*, 1: 21–48.

Holmes, T. H. and Rahe, R. H. (1967) The social readjustment rating scale, *Journal of Psychosomatic Research*, 11: 213–18.

Kennedy, J. A. (1954) *Relax and Live*. London: Rider and Company.

Klarreich, S. L. (1988) *The Stress Solution: How to Be Happier, Healthier and More Effective*. London: Cedar.

Latour, B. (1987) *Science in Action: How to Follow Scientists and Engineers through Society*. Cambridge, MA: Harvard University Press.

Lawson, A. (1978) *Freedom from Stress: Natural Drugless Methods for the Relief of Tension*. Wellingborough: Thorsons.

Looker, T. and Gregson, O. (1989) *Stresswise: A Practical Guide for Dealing with Stress*. Sevenoaks: Hodder & Stoughton.

Madders, J. (1988) *Stress and Relaxtion: Self-help Techniques for Everyone*. London: Optima.

Martin, E. (1994) *Flexible Bodies: Tracking Immunity in American Culture from the Days of Polio to the Age of AIDS*. Boston: Beacon Press.

Meichenbaum, D. (1983) *Coping with Stress*. London: Century.

Norfolk, D. (1979) *The Stress Factor*. London: Hamlyn.

Patel, C. (1992) Foreword. In Consumers' Association *Understanding Stress*. London: Hodder & Stoughton.

Potter, J. and Wetherell, M. (1987) *Discourse and Social Psychology: Beyond Attitudes and Behaviour*. London: Sage.

Powell, K. (1993) *Burnout: What Happens When Stress Gets Out of Control and How to Regain Your Sanity*. London: Thorsons.

Rabinbach, A. (1990) *The Human Motor: Energy, Fatigue and the Origins of Modernity*. Berkeley: University of California Press.

Rabinow, P. (1992) Artificiality and enlightenment: from sociobiology to biosociality. In J. Crary and S. Kwinter (eds) *Zone 6: Incorporations*. New York: Zone.

Rorie, R. A. B. (1968) *Do Something about Those Nerves*. London: Tandem.

Rosch, P. J. (1995) Is hysteria catching? Don't blame it all on 'stress', *Stress Medicine*, 11(2): 71–4.

Rose, N. (1989) *Governing the Soul: The Shaping of the Private Self*. London: Routledge.

Rose, N. (1996) *Inventing the Self*. Cambridge: Cambridge University Press.

Silva, J. and Goldman, B. (1988) *The Silva Mind Control Method of Mental Dynamicas*. London: Grafton.

Stainton Rogers, W. (1991) *Explaining Health and Illness: An Exploration of Diversity*. Hemel Hempstead: Harvester Wheatsheaf.

Stenner, P. (1993) Discoursing jealousy. In E. Burman and I. Parker (eds) *Discourse Analytic Research: Repertoires and Readings of Texts in Action*. London: Routledge.

Stenner, P. and Eccleston, C. (1994) On the textuality of being: towards an invigorated social constructionism, *Theory and Psychology*, 4(1): 85–101.

Stresscheck (1992) Worcestershire: Berean Projects.

Thompson, R. (1982) *Pocket Guide to Stress*. London: Arlington.

Thrift, N. (1997) Soft capitalism, *Cultural Values*, 1(1): 29–57.

Trauer, T. (1986) *Coping with Stress*. London: Salamander.

White, M. (1992) *Tele-advising: Therapeutic Discourse in American Television*. Chapel Hill: University of North Carolina Press.

Wilson, P. (1997) *The Little Book of Calm*. Harmondsworth: Penguin.

Young, A. (1980) The discourse on stress and the reproduction of conventional knowledge, *Social Science and Medicine*, 148: 133–46.

# 3 'It's your opportunity to be truthful': disbelief, mundane reasoning and the investigation of crime

## TIMOTHY AUBURN, SUSAN LEA AND SUSAN DRAKE

### Introduction

The administrative apparatuses of modern society, such as the criminal justice system, form a powerful backdrop to individuals' action, structuring a field of relations and potentials for legitimate and illegitimate action in everyday encounters (Giddens 1986). Within the criminal justice system, the police service is the main organization which has the authority to control citizens' actions in relation to the law and to investigate citizens when suspected of breaking the law. Pursuing an investigation inevitably involves interviewing the suspects of a crime.

### A recent history of police interviewing research in the UK

It has long been recognized that one of the dangers of questioning people under duress is the increased likelihood of a false confession (Kassin 1997).

Concern over this matter led to the setting up of a Royal Commission on Criminal Procedure (1981) which focused on police practices that may affect the reliability of the information obtained during police interviews (e.g. Morris 1980).

In one of the major projects undertaken for the Commission, Irving (1980a, b; Hilgendorf and Irving 1981) drew upon the extant social psychological literature in developing a framework for understanding the police suspect interviewing situation (e.g. social influence research, obedience research). He developed a decision-making model which conceived of the suspect as a rational decision-maker who is concerned to maximize positive outcomes based on the information available and the perceived outcomes of different courses of action. False confessions can arise when a suspect makes a decision to say something incriminating in the belief that this will lead to the best outcome in the immediate circumstances. The belief that a 'confession' is the best course of action is influenced by the circumstances of detention and by the information that the police have selectively imparted during questioning. This decision-making model formed a basis for a powerful critique of police interviewing practices, especially when allied to Irving's participant observational study at a Brighton police station.

Following the Police and Criminal Evidence Act 1984, which implemented a number of the commission's recommendations, two further significant models of police interviewing emerged: interrogative suggestibility and ethical interviewing. The interrogative suggestibility model (Gudjonsson and Clark 1986; Gudjonsson 1992) was based largely on a clinical understanding of a suspect's vulnerability to the unique pressures of being interviewed by the police. The ethical interviewing model (Shepherd 1986, 1991; Shepherd and Kite 1988, 1989) was based on a social skills model, and focused on educating the police in practices which avoided coercive strategies and recognized the limitations of a suspect's ability to tell. These research programmes have in turn led the police service to revise its training and recommended procedures for interviewing suspects (Williamson 1993).

There are two main assumptions central to psychological approaches to police interviewing: an individualistic conceptualization of the problems of interviewing and an adherence to a subjective/objective distinction in accounts. The implication that a significant component of the problems associated with police interviewing lies with the individual's psychological make-up is reflected in a widely accepted typology of false confessions (Kassin and Wrightsman 1985). This typology identifies three false confessions: voluntary, coerced compliant and coerced internalized. A voluntary false confession is offered in the absence of any attempt at elicitation. A coerced compliant confession involves public acquiescence in order to obtain an immediate instrumental gain. A coerced internalized confession occurs when through the process of interrogation the suspect comes to believe the false account of the crime which he or she is under pressure to produce.

These types of false confession, in particular the latter two, reflect the individualistic concerns of the two theories of false confession outlined above. Thus the coerced compliant false confession reflects the situationally produced irrationality of the suspect and the internalized false confession reflects a concern with the overly suggestible individual who internalizes a police version of events. This assumption has led to a significant body of research which attempts to identify the sorts of vulnerabilities that might lead an individual to confess falsely, e.g. drug intoxication or mental characteristics (Gudjonsson 1994; Pearse 1995).

The second assumption is the focus for the approach taken here. Psychological approaches have assumed that there are two sorts of account that can be given of an event. First, there is a subjective account which is biased insofar as it arises from a distorted recall or telling of events. The accuracy of this account can be determined through comparison of its details with those given in the second sort of account. This second account is objective and value-free, representing the events in a factual and undistorted way. This assumption underlies the recent distinction between interrogation and investigative interviewing (Williamson 1994). Interrogation is subject to a range of biases. In addition to the vulnerabilities of the suspect, there are also the attitudes and expectations of the police when conducting the interviews, in particular the perception by the police that the main purpose of interviewing suspects is to obtain a confession and thereby confirm the guilt of the suspect (Holdaway 1983; Mortimer 1992, 1994). In contrast, in investigative interviewing the police are encouraged to adopt strategies which minimize the introduction of biased information, and which allow the suspect an opportunity to explain in his or her own terms the alleged criminal events (e.g. Shepherd 1991).

The objection to the assumption of a subjective/objective distinction is based on the observation of wide variation in the sorts of descriptions that can be given for an event. It is therefore difficult to isolate one description of events as an objectively neutral one against which other versions can be compared. For example, descriptions of an event as murder, a shooting or pulling the trigger of a handgun are all conceivably accurate descriptions but differ in their implications about what happened and the blameworthiness of the characters involved (Wagenaar *et al.* 1993). Rather than attempting to isolate an objective description of the events, it is more appropriate to consider descriptions or versions for the inferences they provide about the events they represent and how they construct the motives and interests of the people involved. Descriptions both construct the world and are themselves constructed from the resources available to the person. Potter (1996) argues that the events cannot be specified prior to or separately from the context or activity which generates the description. Consequently, it is necessary to examine descriptions of events as a social practice: that is to say, how participants in the course of social interaction 'turn descriptions into facts and how they stabilize and reify versions of the world as just how things are' (Potter 1996: 205).

## Discourse analytic approach

Discursive approaches to the area of police interviewing have challenged these assumptions and in so doing advocated a systematic process-oriented evaluation of interviewing (see Watson 1983, 1990; McConville *et al.* 1991). We have followed the principles of discursive psychology (Edwards and Potter 1992), in which there is a focus on the discursive activities of the participants in an encounter and how these activities contribute to its developing and shifting meaning. This focus emphasizes the occasioned nature of talk and hence its functional orientation. The three main principles by which a discourse analytic approach proceeds are: variability, construction and function (Potter and Wetherell 1987). Thus there is an active search for instances in which particular objects or events are talked about in different or variable ways. Then, the manner in which these variable versions of events are constructed is analysed. Finally, the functional orientation and how the participants take up and display their inferences from these variable constructions is examined. In the context of police interviewing this approach translates into a set of more specific considerations.

First, whatever 'really happened', there are a variety of versions of the event which can be recounted. Different versions will select particular actions or features of the event, or construct aspects of them in certain ways which allow for inferences about the role and responsibility of the characters involved. There is also likely to be more than one version of the events available, so that the implied inferences of the different versions become a point of contention between the participants. Agreeing to a particular version will have material and legal consequences for the suspect and possibly the police officer too.

A second consideration is the observation that the institutional context of the police interview renders a particular version of events as salient to the participants. This particular version can be labelled the 'preferred version' (Auburn *et al.* 1995). This term is not intended to convey the notion that this version is one that is preferred in a psychological sense, but that it is institutionally facilitated. This version of events is one that progresses the business of doing justice and policing and thus is oriented to by the participants.

The preferred version articulates a particular version of the alleged crime:

1 A certain content (that certain things happened in a certain way), where this content is treated for practical purposes as an objective description of events.
2 A certain agentic position for the suspect within these events.

The elements of the preferred version correspond broadly to the legal considerations of *actus reus* (i.e. that certain acts occurred) and *mens rea* (i.e. that there was criminal intention) (Seago 1994). The 'preferred version' therefore constructs the suspect or accomplice as guilty of the offence and facilitates the functioning of the criminal justice system in disposing of suspects.

## Police interviewing and intersubjectivity

One of the main activities of police interviews with suspects is the business of achieving agreement over what 'really happened'. Thus, in an interview, it is not practical as a way of progressing the criminal justice system simply for the police to state one version of events and for suspects to state a radically divergent version of events. This situation would breach two assumptions of social interaction: intersubjectivity and mundane reason. One useful definition of intersubjectivity is offered by Billig: 'the assumption of intersubjectivity is a basic assumption of social life; everyday reasoning assumes that viewpoints should be substitutable for each other and that non-substitutable viewpoints are seen to constitute a threat to the assumption of the reality of the world, and therefore differences between viewpoints need to be accounted for' (Billig 1991: 170). The notion of mundane reason follows directly from this assumption of intersubjectivity:

> both everyday and sociological discourse, practice and inquiry are dependent upon assumptions about the nature of 'objective reality', to wit that there is an objective determinate order independent of the acts of observation or description through which it is known. The assumption of an 'out there', 'public' or 'objective' world is a central feature of a network of beliefs about reality, self and others which comprise what I shall call mundane reason. For most Western adults, the assumption of an objective reality is virtually self-evident (and thus truly mundane).
>
> (Pollner 1987: ix–x)

The stipulation of an objective reality is the main assumption of mundane reason. Another assumption is the distinction between an objective and subjective realm. Further, mundane reason stipulates that objects, events and processes in the outer, objective realm are determinate, coherent and non-contradictory. Consequently, the accounts and experiences of mundane reasoners should reflect this stipulated realm of objective reality: that is, their accounts will also be determinate, coherent and compatible. One possibility which Pollner specifically raises is where mundane reasoners disagree in their accounts of the (assumed) objective realm; such discrepancies (or disjunctive experiences) between reasoners are accountable matters and he argues that reasoners then search for how such a discrepancy could have occurred given the coherency and determinateness of the public domain. He goes on to suggest that occasions of apparent reality disjuncture are resolvable by drawing upon accounting devices which claim that they are the product of 'exceptional methods of observation, experience or reportage' (Pollner 1987: 69). Such devices might include claims of impaired sight or hearing, or that one of the mundane reasoners was joking, using metaphor or lying.

The interrelated notions of intersubjectivity and mundane reason are especially relevant to police interviewing, where one person, the suspect, is specifically and explicitly held accountable for her or his version of events. What we wish to explore are those occasions when such reality disjunctures occur in the interviews, how they are dealt with and their implications for the status of the suspect. Intersubjectivity and mundane reasoning can be treated as both a difficulty and a resource for participants. It is a difficulty insofar as discrepancies between versions of reality have to be resolved in some way; it is a resource insofar as it allows one of the parties (usually the police officer) to require the other to account for the discrepancy. In the analysis to follow we have operationalized these reality disjunctures as occasions where disbelief is expressed.

## Method of analysis

A number of officially recorded interviews between police officers and suspects were available. This analysis was based on eight fully transcribed interviews selected randomly from the collection. Since the interviews were recorded prior to the Criminal Justice and Public Disorder Act 1994, there was in principle a right to silence for the suspects. However, so-called 'no comment' interviews were not included. All the interviewers were male police officers and all but one of the suspects was male. In only one of the interviews was there a third party present; in this interview the third party was an appropriate adult since the suspect was a juvenile. The types of crime of which the suspects were accused were mainly theft or crimes involving physical assault. The analysis proceeded with the authors reading through the transcripts with the aim of identifying instances of reality disjuncture. This first reading was inclusive, so that doubtful or marginal instances were identified. A broad working definition of reality disjuncture was to identify a participant's orientation to non-substitutable versions of 'objective reality' in which disbelief was expressed by one speaker about a version of events supplied by another speaker.

These instances of disbelief were then subjected to detailed analysis and interpretation. The aim of this part of the analysis was to identify ways in which the extracts were discursively organized and their functional orientation. The range of rhetorical devices used to achieve certain effects was identified. The semantic content of talk was also examined in order to understand how elements of more widely distributed social knowledge were deployed again as means of achieving certain effects. This latter aspect of the analysis has been characterized as the search for social and ideological constructions which permeate the text and which facilitate the achievement of relational effects within the interaction order. As a group we then met and discussed each extract with the aim of reaching agreement regarding its interpretation. This stage of the analysis was an iterative process so that there were several meetings at which interpretations were rediscussed and new ideas incorporated. The analysis and discussion here represent a provisional agreement about our interpretation of this corpus of material.

## Analysis

It is self-evident that the criminal justice system does not allow a person to be guilty of a crime and simultaneously not guilty of the same crime; thus there cannot be competing versions of the same event with these contradictory positions for the suspect which are both endorsed by the criminal justice system. As Pollner (1987) has shown, the criminal justice system is strongly committed to the stipulations of mundane reason. Thus there has to be an effort directed towards disambiguation when the criminal justice system, through its agents, encounters competing versions of an event or, in Pollner's terminology, a reality disjuncture.

### Discursive organization of disbelief

When one of the participants wishes to register disagreement with a version previously supplied by another, then this disagreement is frequently expressed as disbelief. As such, disbelief is marked and oriented to as identifying a problematic feature of the way the interview is progressing. This analysis indicated that we could formulate an 'ideal' discursive organization for the expression of disbelief. This ideal organization had three parts.

1 Directly or indirectly signalling or asserting disbelief on the part of the current speaker in response to an assertion or set of assertions made by a prior speaker (signalling disbelief).
2 Warranting the expression of disbelief by drawing attention to 'factual' matters from which there is an available inference of some inconsistent states of the world (warranting disbelief).
3 Concluding the disbelief and creating the expectation of a reformulated version on the part of the prior speaker consistent with the state of the world constructed by the 'disbelieving' speaker (reformulation invitation).

*Signalling disbelief*

In the following extract (Extract 1), a woman has been accused of assaulting her partner and seriously injuring him.

**Extract 1 (AF/3678/3)$_1$**

| 1 | PO1: | [susname] you are (.) |
|---|---|---|
| 2 | | I believe first that you're not actually being |
| 3 | | honest with your self and with us |
| 4 | | in fact I don't believe that you're actually |
| 5 | | telling the truth |
| | | |
| 6 | I: | I am telling you the truth |
| | | |
| 7 | PO1: | Now [namea] has been stabbed twice |
| 8 | | and he's been bitten on the nose |
| | | |
| 9 | I: | Yeah |
| | | |
| 10 | PO1: | He's in hospital now |
| | | |
| 11 | I: | mmmh |
| | | |
| 12 | PO1: | I believe that you are the person who have |
| 13 | | actually inflicted those stab wounds to [namea] |
| 14 | | now think carefully (.) and answer the question |
| 15 | | honestly |
| | | |
| 16 | I: | No I didn't do it |

The three-part organization can be identified in this extract. The first part (lines 1–5) corresponds to signalling disbelief. This part has a reflexive quality. It functions as commentary on the processes that have occurred up to that point in the interview; more specifically, it evaluates the conduct of the suspect herself. This evaluation corresponds to one of the devices which Pollner identified as a means of maintaining a commitment to mundane reason, i.e. discounting the quality of the description of events provided by the suspect. One of the noticeable features of this instance of signalling disbelief is that it is composed of two parts. The first part has an affiliative quality. It accuses the suspect not only of being dishonest with the (institutional) 'us' (line 3) but also of engaging in self-deception. This accusation draws upon a psychotherapeutic discourse; it claims a privileged status for the accuser (therapist) in being able to discern a motivation for the suspect's (patient's) behaviour. It thus draws attention to the distinction between a subjective, biased account and an objective account. Second, this accusation draws further upon a psychotherapeutic discourse by affiliating both the police officer and the suspect potentially to a joint project of overcoming this self-deception.

The second part upgrades the accusation by replacing the hedged and indirect accusation in the first part with a more direct accusation of lying (lines 4–5). This part makes what can be termed a 'bottom-line' ontological claim: that is, to an absolute version of events glossed here as 'the truth'. Such a claim asserts that there is available a description of the event which is objective and unambiguous, and into which the known 'facts' will fit consistently as a coherent story line. Accusing a speaker of 'not telling the truth' is to imply that the accuser is in possession of information which within the conventional norms of storytelling about real events – that is, within the stipulations of mundane reason – creates an inconsistency. Moreover, it implies that the accuser knows that the speaker is also aware of this inconsistent information and is deliberately withholding or distorting it. Making this assertion therefore signals the inadequacy of the suspect's account. Taken together, these two parts make explicit the problems of a reality disjuncture, and that such problems require resolution. The inference is that there are two versions of the events being endorsed: there is one version endorsed by the suspect and there is another which has an objective unassailable property, glossed as the 'truth'. Drawing upon bottom-line assertions of 'truth' privileges this version and indicates that the version to which the suspect has aligned herself should be amended in some way.

*Warranting disbelief*

The second part to the expression of disbelief is a warrant (lines 7–10). The suspect has straightforwardly denied or contradicted the police officer's assertion of dishonesty. The police officer marks his next response (line 7: 'Now . . .'), which can be heard as marking a dispreferred second and thereby as addressing the contradictory claim made by the suspect. The subsequent warrant for the disagreement is achieved through a particular construction of the events constituting the suspect's assault on her partner. The rhetorical device deployed for constructing a version of these events is a three-part list (stabbed twice; bitten on the nose; is in hospital). This list serves to link together the events and the seriousness of the consequences. Moreover, they are linked by being drawn from a 'disorderly discourse of violence' (Auburn *et al.* 1995). It identifies events that are consistent with illegitimate violence, using direct action terms ('stab', 'bite') which allow an inference of actions of an extreme, uncontrolled character perpetrated by the suspect. The use of the passive voice ('[namea] has been stabbed') indicates that the victim had actions inflicted upon him, and thus did not have any agentic role in producing such injuries. In addition, the level of harm is implied in the third part of the list, where the officer describes the end state of the victim as being hospitalized. This construction sets up a 'puzzle' about the identity of the agent who did inflict the injuries and draws attention to features of the account previously supplied by the suspect that require further accounting.

*Reformulation invitation*

There are potentially different methods available for resolving this disjuncture. One would be for the suspect to amend her own version. Another option is displayed here in the third part of the expression of disbelief (reformulation invitation; lines 12–15). Here the police officer draws explicit inferences about how the suspect's version should be altered to resolve the 'puzzle' heard in the previous part. The police officer accuses the suspect of stabbing the victim (lines 12–13), thus identifying the agent who perpetrated the violence upon the victim as the suspect. The 'puzzle' resolution is followed by an invitation to the suspect to give a response. However, this invitation is constructed in such a way as to create a number of expectations about the character of this response. First, there is the injunction to 'think carefully', which can be heard as an instruction to the suspect to consider her response in terms of the expression of disbelief and the evidence which warranted it. Second, the content of the response is indicated in the invocation to respond 'honestly'. The term 'answering honestly' mirrors the phrase used in the first part (signalling disbelief), in which the suspect was accused of not 'telling the truth' (line 5). The invocation thus excludes the suspect's original version as an optional answer and privileges a revised version which is consistent with the details supplied by the police officer.

Another feature of the overall organization of the expression of disbelief concerns the options for responding on the part of the suspect. There are potentially insertion points available for the suspect to interrupt the development of the expression of disbelief; these insertion points appear to be located at the end of each of the component parts of the overall expression. Thus, at the end of the first part (signalling disbelief) both police officer and suspect are oriented to a response from the suspect. At the end of the second and third parts to the expression there are also potential insertion points for the suspect. These insertion points are taken up by the suspect but it is noticeable that the response denies the implicit expectations of the police officer's formulation of the suspect's story and reasserts the quality of original story line (e.g. 'I am telling the truth'). The development of the expression of disbelief can be heard as successive upgradings of disbelief as the suspect responds in a way that sustains the disjuncture between the two versions of events.

## Effects of the expression of disbelief

This analysis suggests that the expression of disbelief is designed here as a persuasive device. Disbelief is constructed as an evaluation of the acceptability of the version of events that has been supplied by the suspect. The expression of disbelief is an instance where, within the local context of an interview, the suspect's accountability is made evident. Further, this accountability is achieved by utilizing the common-sense assumptions concerning intersubjectivity and mundane reason. By drawing upon bottom-line claims about 'truth', an expectation of a single agreed upon account which has a status independent of the observer or teller of it is displayed as a matter of concern by the police officer. This concern about the lack of intersubjective agreement on 'what really happened' is warranted by a particular selection of features of the event which give rise to inferences that there are discrepancies between the two available versions. The production of a discrepancy in turn relies upon carefully crafted fact construction so that the discrepancy becomes a plausible inference from the selection and meaning of the 'facts' as part of a wider narrative of events. The persuasive element of the expression of disbelief takes its force from the reformulation of events that is expected and displayed in the third part of the overall organization. This part expresses clearly the narrative or version that would resolve the reality disjuncture, and sustain the assumption of an intersubjectively agreed reality, by privileging one version aligned with the police and the criminal justice system (the preferred version) and denying the version articulated by the suspect.

## Methods of warranting disbelief

In the analysis of this three-part organization of the expression of disbelief, one of the major areas of variation was in the methods utilized by the participants for warranting their disbelief.

### Witness information

One of the ways in which disbelief was warranted was through the utilization of witness information (see Extract 2).

### Extract 2 (AF/3674)

```
 1  PO1:  (1) errm (.) see the bottom line is
 2         as far as I'm concerned
 3         I don't actually believe what you're saying
 4         errm I've got someone who's got nothing to gain
 5         nothing to lose
 6         a member of the public has come to us
 7         called us up
 8         we come down
 9         identified you to
10         your clothing to a tee
```

11          the description he gave could only have
12          only been one person in [cityname]
13          and that was you
14          okay you've now admitted you were there
15          you acted as a lookout that's what you said
16          this chap's turned round and said
17          the chap in the black leather jacket
18          and for the benefit of the tape
19          [susname] is wearing a black leather jacket
20          at this moment in time
21          was holding a screwdriver
22          while [namea] was hitting half a brick on to
23          the head of a screwdriver in towards
24          or on to the meter

25  PO2:    Then he went into more depth
26          he said that every time somebody walked past
27          you jumped into the doorway
28          you even threw the screwdriver and the brick
29          underneath a car that was parked at the meter
30          and went back again and picked it up

31  PO1:    You know these things are true

In this extract, a strong assertion of disbelief is initially formulated (lines 1–3). This signalling of disbelief evaluates the story that the suspect has previously provided and indicates that for the police officer the story is inadequate in some unspecified respects. This part is followed by an extended version of the circumstances which warrant this disbelief and so can be heard as identifying the particulars of the story that are inadequate. This version is composed as a 'footed' report (Clayman 1992). The police officers were not the actual witnesses to the events, but are in the position of reanimating it. There are two noticeable features of the way that this footed report is organized. First, there is an orientation to the possible stake of the witness in reporting these events to the police. Second, there is an orientation to the accuracy of the information that the witness has given through the use of fine-grained detail in the reported events.

The stake of a witness is an important consideration for participants in assessing the status of a report (see Edwards and Potter 1993). If a witness report can be demonstrated to be motivated by an interest of some sort then the information that this witness is assumed to impart can be argued to be discountable. The police officers in this sequence from the interview take care to display quite explicitly that the witness has not been motivated to give the report of the event because of any personally relevant outcome (lines 4–5), and this disinterestedness of the witness in giving the report is supplemented by the information that the witness approached the police himself (lines 6–8). By selecting this information about the appearance of the witness, the police can be heard to imply that they have not had a role in eliciting a report that may be detrimental to the suspect. Therefore the status of the witness as independent, in the sense of both having no self-interest and providing information without police prompting, suggests an authenticity to the report.

The second feature of this reanimation of the witness report is the finely grained detail that is presented. First, the police officer claims that the witness's description of the clothing was so detailed that it fitted those of the suspect and no other person among the population of a large city (lines 9–13). The consistency between the witness's description of the clothing and the clothing that the suspect has on is then displayed more explicitly by referring to the 'black leather jacket' (lines 16–20). Second, the police officers describe quite minutely the specific actions of the suspect that taken together can be heard as a suspiciously criminal act (lines 21–30). The orientation to the detail is displayed in the comment that one police officer makes upon the report of the witness that it was a report which went 'into more depth' (line 25). This reanimation of the detail warrants the actions as authentically having taken place.

Taken together, these two devices for reanimating the witness report indicate that there is a discrepancy between the version provided by the suspect and that which is implicitly the preferred version privileged by the police officer. This discrepancy, between the suspect's version and that which is 'factually' available, undermines the assumption of intersubjectivity. The police officers have drawn attention to a reality disjuncture which requires resolution. The consequence for the suspect is that he is subsequently expected to resolve this reality disjuncture and is therefore accountable for the version that he has provided. The final part to the expression of disbelief is an evaluation precisely of the witness's report and the status of the information that it imparts (line 31). Here the police officer states that the events described by the witness are to be heard and treated in a particular way. He evaluates the witness's description as 'true', thus privileging this description as the preferred version of events.

### Indisputable sources of evidence

Another way in which police officers can warrant their disbelief at the version offered by a suspect is to draw upon an actual or potential record of evidence which is formulated as foundational and indisputable. In the following extract the police officer makes two consecutive expressions of disbelief, and both times warrants these expressions by reference to the sort of indisputable evidence that a scientist could produce.

**Extract 3 (AF/3678/4)**

```
 1   PO1:   (1) are you (.)
 2           as the sergeant said
 3           to be quite honest we don't believe what you're
 4           telling us
 5           do you understand that things like blood staining
 6           on clothing can be put to a scientist
 7           very clever people
 8           and they can prove whose blood that is
 9           and as the sergeant pointed out when he showed
10           you the trousers
11           the amount of blood is not consistent with a
12           scratch
13           it's a lot of blood
14           now it's your interview
15           and your opportunity if you wish
16           it's your opportunity to be truthful because
17           things might have happened that you haven't told
18           us all about that might be in your favour
19           do you understand what I'm saying

20   I:      mmm

21   PO1:    Yeah

22   I:      Yeah

23   PO1:    But the story you've given us first of all is not
24           consistent with the story that we've already had
25           from him initially
26           and obviously we can put things like your
27           trousers to a scientist
28           and just think what people like that can say
29           he can say whose blood that is
30           he can quantify how much blood there is
31           there are all sorts of things (0.7)
32           and the story you're telling us now isn't
33           going to look very good in the future when things
34           like that are put against scientists and things
35           is it
36           because you know what happened
37           you were there
38           and you're the only one who can tell us
39           yeah

40   I:      mmm but I'm telling the truth
```

In this extract there are two expressions of disbelief (lines 1–19; 23–39). As in previous extracts, these expressions begin with a clear assertion of disbelief (lines 3–4 and lines 23–25), although the second expression is a downgraded assertion compared to the first. In both expressions the warrant for the disbelief is achieved by drawing attention to the inconsistency between the version provided by the suspect and that which is available from a version potentially supplied by a 'scientist'. The police officer warrants a preferred version by utilizing category entitlement as a rhetorical device: that is, people are assigned to certain categories and are then assumed or expected to possess certain knowledge or skills as members of that category. Thus the police officer formulates scientists as 'very clever people' (line 7) and as having available the resources and ability to determine the source and quantity of blood found at the scene of the crime. This ability to determine such 'facts of the matter' is identified through a three-part list (lines 29–31) which upgrades and legitimizes the information that such 'scientists' can provide. Here, then, the police officer is concerned to challenge the version of events that the suspect has provided and to provide an indication of the available alternative version which the police officer can establish as the consensual version of events. This alternative version is privileged and warranted through the formulation of the status of scientists which legitimizes this version as based on foundational and indisputable knowledge.

### Normative expectations

The final warrant that we wish to identify is one based upon normative expectations. Having expressed disbelief, police officers will sometimes warrant this disbelief by characterizing a situation from which certain normative expectations about how a person would behave follow.

### Extract 4 (AF/3674/8)

```
 1  PO1:  I'm not convinced that he would stop half through
 2         breaking into a parking meter to go home have his
 3         dinner and speak to his mum

 4  I:     Nah because he went out this morning
 5         what time did he knock knock for me mum this
 6         morning

 7  AA:    I can't remember (susname)

 8  I:     He knocked early about nine o'clock erm
 9         and come round to me
10         and then I went out with him
11         got the paper for his mum
12         went his house
```

```
13              gave the paper to his mum
14              then we went out
15    PO:       Yeah I can see what you are saying
16              but if you're doing something
17              writing a letter or if you were
18              don't know do you have any hobbies
19              if you were playing football
20              you wouldn't stop halfway through your game of
21              football and think I haven't seen me mum all day
22              I better go home and have something to eat
23              was there a reason why you stopped half way
24              through
25              was it the police arriving was it us arriving
26              or was it somebody else walking down the street
27              I don't see why you would suddenly stop half way
28              through
```

In this extract the police officer remarks that he cannot accept the version of events offered by the suspect. As part of initially signalling his disbelief he also formulates a summary of the suspect's version of events. This summary selects certain events from the suspect's previous version and places them in a narrative sequence from which an implausibility can be inferred. This summary is elaborated after the suspect has supplied an alternative narrative sequence which is designed to solve the implausibility implicit in the police officer's summary version. This elaboration draws more explicitly on expectations of how people normally behave and identifies what would therefore be regarded as a puzzling exception to such norms. In elaborating this breach of normative expectations the police officer displays more clearly the assumptions contained in his initial warrant to his disbelief. He draws out an analogy between 'breaking into a parking meter' (line 2) and a 'game of football' (lines 20–21). It is expected that in the normal course of events, once embarked upon a game such as football, the participants play according to a set of rules which includes its beginning and end. The implausibility is achieved by then suggesting that such games might be abandoned when a participant had a sudden wish to see his mother and to eat. It seems, then, that the analogy between the criminal act ('breaking into a parking meter') and the football game relies upon hearing both as being self-contained activities which the participant would pursue until completion unless interrupted by events outside the participant's control. This way of achieving such a normative implausibility is reinforced by the observation that the police officer starts with an analogy to 'writing a letter' (line 17) but abandons this analogy in favour of the football game. It is likely that writing a letter can plausibly be interrupted before completion in order to eat or meet another person.

The last part to the disbelief then follows (lines 23–28) from the normative expectations set up by the analogy to the football game, through which the actions in the suspect's version are rendered implausible and inconsistent. The police officer identifies the actions central to this implausibility and asks the suspect to account for them (lines 23–24). The police officer then supplies a set of candidate answers to this question (lines 25–26) which clearly specify elements consistent with a preferred version. This sequence plus the police officer's restatement of the puzzle that warrants the disbelief acts to invite the suspect to supply a reformulation of his version of events either in agreement with or consistent with the police officer's candidate answers.

## Conclusion

This analysis has illustrated how an important aspect of the business of doing justice is conducted at an interactional level which reproduces criminal justice as an administrative system. Disbelief is a resource based in the inter-action order and is used within police interviews as a persuasive device. As a persuasive device it draws upon the assumptions of the interaction order, particularly those of mundane reasoning and the normative requirements to account for reality disjunctures. Within police interviews this requirement to account is situationally manufactured by police officers, who deploy a range of rhetorical devices, notably a well organized device for constructing dis-belief in order to achieve this outcome. The consequence for the suspect is to draw attention to discrepancies between his or her own description of events and the alternative available to the police. It also creates an expecta-tion that the discrepancy should be resolved through an amendment of the suspect's original account. This characterization of the functioning of disbelief also draws attention to its asymmetrical use within police inter-views. Expressions of disbelief are more often utilized by police officers as a persuasive device for marking out the relevant content of the institution-ally preferred version of events, for demonstrating its plausibility and for potentially eliciting agreement to it (see also McConville *et al.* 1991).

At this interactional level the criminal justice system is reproduced, both for the participants in the interview itself and for others who play their role within the system more widely, e.g. prosecutors, juries and lawyers. Hence the ability to account for reality disjunctures, even the plausibility of the disjunctures themselves, will influence the career of the suspect through the criminal justice system. The police interview acts not only as an occasion for 'gathering information' but also, owing to the social organization of that information and the social dynamics of its production, as a rhetorical resource within the criminal justice system in its own right. It functions as resource for holding the main participants accountable for claims made during the interview at later stages of the legal process. For example, not only can suspects be held accountable for the plausibility of the way in which they deal with police officers' production of reality disjunctures (disbelief), but police officers can be held accountable for the manner in which reality disjunctures have been produced (e.g. was it overly coercive or leading?).

In contrast to previous social psychological approaches, which have focused on individual vulnerabilities or particular interviewing strategies, this approach focuses on the joint production of information and its grounding in institutional practices. Further, this analysis indicates how the discursive resources available to the police through their institutional positioning enables a 'preferred' version of events to be made explicit and its plausibility demonstrated despite the lack of agreement of the suspect. This issue has been overlooked by previous psychological approaches to police interviewing, which have focused on the direct effects upon the suspect of police questioning in terms of her or his likelihood of yielding to coercive questioning. This analysis indicates that an equally important consequence of police questioning is to place 'on the record' the institutionally preferred version of events. It also allows for those who later hear the recorded interviews to make judgements about the suspect's ability to deal plausibly with this preferred version.

## Potential for application

This research has not entailed a close liaison with those involved in the police interviews themselves. Thus we have not engaged, for example, with suspects, revealed their stories more fully or their history of involvement with the criminal justice system. However, this research does have some potential for broader application. The principles for such application stem from recent debates about the nature of discourse analysis as a particular manifestation of critical social psychology and its progress as a form of practical intervention. There are those who advocate that discourse analysis should act principally as a wide-ranging critique of social practices. Potter (1997) has argued that discourse analysis can act as a critique of contemporary social practices on three levels: ideological critique, fact critique and disciplinary critique and reflexivity. This approach to intervention is undoubtedly necessary. It leaves unresolved, however, how such critiques would function outside the academy: that is, what criteria can be explicated for placing and engaging such critiques. Consequently, others have argued that, though necessary, this form of intervention is not sufficient. For example, Parker (1997) has argued that practical intervention should be based on criteria concerned with the identification of misused or oppressive psychological practices, and aligning the critique with those who are the objects or patients of such practices. Approaches which call for an intervention based on politically derived criteria have themselves been criticized on two main counts. First, there are a number of assumptions about social structure and processes which remain largely unexplicated in these approaches; second, they tend to overstate the claim that the social practices investigated by discourse analysts are inherently problematic (Potter 1997: 58–9). It follows that there is a need for closely argued contingent application of discourse analytic research to selected contexts where assumptions about the nature of the practice under investigation can be argued through with colleagues and practitioners.

In terms of the present research, criteria about whom to engage with are clearly not based upon an underlying notion of the truth or falsity of accusations of guilt. Criteria for engagement and application are based on moral and political arguments. Accusations of assault, for example, can legally construct the actions of those involved in domestic violence and those involved in anti-government protest as the same category of offence. However, it would be possible to deconstruct the narratives surrounding these offences and to reconstitute them differentially as actions that have little political merit versus actions that have substantial political merit. One proposal is that the findings from this research could be taken up and developed in conjunction with a whole range of groups who are regularly in conflict with the criminal justice system and for whom a police interview is one of the many steps in their social and political regulation. One possibility would be then to work with groups such as gays, civil liberties organizations, mental health organizations, animal rights organizations and trade unionists to develop information packages and training programmes to enable them to resist the positioning of them as offenders when engaged in interviews which attempt to place on record the preferred version of events. This involvement could include identifying those most at risk of arrest and helping to develop strategies for resistance during the interview through, for example, a thorough knowledge of the relevant law and an awareness of the interactional devices used in interviews to construct a plausible preferred version. Developments of this sort may be doubly urgent as the longstanding right to silence when being questioned by the police has now been abolished in English Law (Royal Commission on Criminal Justice 1993).

Second, the application or take-up of such proposals as they emanate from discourse analytic work itself becomes the object of further discourse analytic work. Since meanings shift, since the intentions of the author have been largely erased as a legitimate object of analysis and since the domain of application is part of the research cycle, there is a need to incorporate evaluation of that application into the research enterprise. For discourse analytically inspired application to policy or for particular groups, there is no guarantee about the outcomes of that application. Evaluation therefore becomes an issue of undertaking further discursive analysis. This requirement has been elaborated as follows:

> I would argue that, far from being futile and circular, this sort of reflexivity is required if we are to critically address our own constructions of the social world, our own constructions of what is radical and what is reactionary, and the authority relations produced by our own texts. The alternative would be to claim a special privilege: a position beyond the sorts of questioning and criticism that our research participants undergo.
>
> (Potter 1997: 63)

We have tried to show here how the business of doing justice is managed by those caught up in its administrative procedures, and how in so doing, the participants use everyday discursive resources. By adhering to a 'working consensus' which constructs the roles associated with the criminal justice system, the participants actively reproduce the dynamics of a police interview. One of the main effects is to allow different versions of the events to be articulated and for the police to be able to fashion discursively a preferred version of events that will be available to other actors in the criminal justice system. One focus for applying this research is in enabling certain participants to resist their positioning within this preferred version.

## Notes

For purposes of anonymity/confidentiality all references to names and locations have been deleted. The convention followed here is to substitute such names and locations with general labels [namea], [streetnameb] etc. The label [susname] is always used when the suspect is referred to by name in the interview. Speakers are identified as follows: PO(number) – Police officer; I – Interviewee; AA – Appropriate adult.

## References

Auburn, T., Drake, S. and Willig, C. (1995) 'You punched him, didn't you?': versions of violence in accusatory interviews, *Discourse and Society*, 6: 353–86.

Billig, M. (1991) *Ideology and Opinions: Studies in Rhetorical Psychology*. London: Sage Publications.

Clayman, S. E. (1992) Footing in the achievement of neutrality: the case of news-interview discourse. In P. Drew and J. Heritage (eds) *Talk at Work: Interaction in Institutional Settings*. Cambridge: Cambridge University Press.

Edwards, D. and Potter, J. (1992) *Discursive Psychology*. London: Sage.

Edwards, D. and Potter, J. (1993) Language and causation: a discursive action model of description and attribution, *Psychological Review*, 100: 23–41.

Giddens, A. (1986) *Sociology: A Brief but Critical Introduction*. London: Macmillan.

Gudjonsson, G. H. (1992) *The Psychology of Interrogations, Confessions and Testimony*. Chichester: John Wiley and Sons.

Gudjonsson, G. H. (1994) Psychological vulnerability: suspects at risk. In D. Morgan and G. M. Stephenson (eds) *Suspicion and Silence: The Right to Silence in Criminal Investigations*. London: Blackstone Press.

Gudjonsson, G. H. and Clark, N. K. (1986) Suggestibility in police interrogation: a social psychological model, *Social Behaviour*, 1: 83–104.

Hilgendorf, E. L. and Irving, B. (1981) A decision-making model of confessions. In S. Lloyd-Bostock (ed.) *Law and Psychology: Papers Presented at SSRC Law and Psychology Conferences 1979–80*. Oxford: SSRC.

Holdaway, S. (1983) *Inside the British Police: A Force at Work*. Oxford: Blackwell.

Irving, B. (1980a) *Police Interrogation: The Psychological Approach*, Research Study No. 1, Royal Commission on Criminal Procedure. London: HMSO.

Irving, B. (1980b) *Police Interrogation: A Case Study of Current Practice*, Research Study No. 2, Royal Commission on Criminal Procedure. London: HMSO.

Kassin, S. M. (1997) The psychology of confession evidence, *American Psychologist*, 52: 221–33.

Kassin, S. M. and Wrightsman, L. S. (1985) Confession evidence. In S. M. Kassin and L. S. Wrightsman (eds) *The Psychology of Evidence and Trial Procedure*. London: Sage.

McConville, M., Sanders, A. and Leng, R. (1991) *The Case for the Prosecution: Police Suspects and the Construction of Criminality*. London: Routledge.

Morris, P. (1980) *Police Interrogation: Review of Literature*, Research Study No. 3, Royal Commission on Criminal Procedure. London: HMSO.

Mortimer, A. (1992) Why did you do it?, *Policing*, 8: 103–18.

Mortimer, A. (1994) Asking the right questions, *Policing*, 10: 111–24.

Parker, I. (1997) The unconscious state of social psychology. In T. Ibáñez and L. Íñiguez (eds) *Critical Social Psychology*. London: Sage.

Pearse, J. (1995) Police interviewing: the identification of vulnerabilities, *Journal of Community and Applied Social Psychology*, 5: 147–59.

Pollner, M. (1987) *Mundane Reason: Reality in Everyday and Sociological Discourse*. Cambridge: Cambridge University Press.

Potter, J. (1996) *Representing Reality: Discourse, Rhetoric and Social Constructionism*. London: Sage.

Potter, J. (1997) Discourse and critical social psychology. In T. Ibáñez and L. Íñiguez (eds) *Critical Social Psychology*. London: Sage.

Potter, J. and Wetherell, M. (1987) *Discourse and Social Psychology: Beyond Attitudes and Behaviour*. London: Sage.

Royal Commission on Criminal Justice (1993) *Report of the Committee*, Cmnd 2263. London: HMSO.

Royal Commission on Criminal Procedure (1981) *Report of the Committee*, Cmnd 8092. London: HMSO.

Seago, P. (1994) *Criminal Law*, 4th edn. London: Sweet and Maxwell.

Shepherd, E. (1986) Conversational core of policing, *Policing*, 2(4): 294–303.

Shepherd, E. (1991) Ethical interviewing, *Policing*, 7(1): 42–60.

Shepherd, E. and Kite, F. (1988) Training to interview, *Policing*, 4(4): 264–80.

Shepherd, E. and Kite, F. (1989) Teach 'em to talk, *Policing*, 5(1): 33–47.

Wagenaar, W. A., van Koppen, P. J. and Crombag, H. F. M. (1993) *Anchored Narratives: The Psychology of Criminal Evidence*. Hemel Hempstead: Harvester Wheatsheaf.

Watson, D. R. (1983) The presentation of victim and motive in discourse: the case of police interrogations and interviews, *Victimology: An International Journal*, 8: 31–52.

Watson, D. R. (1990) Some features of the elicitation of confessions in murder interrogations. In G. Psathas (ed.) *Interaction Competence*. Maryland: University of America Press.

Williamson, T. M. (1993) From interrogation to investigative interviewing; strategic trends in police questioning, *Journal of Community and Applied Social Psychology*, 3: 89–99.

Williamson, T. (1994) Reflections on current police practice. In D. Morgan and G. M. Stephenson (eds) *Suspicion and Silence: The Right to Silence in Criminal Investigations*. London: Blackstone Press.

# 4 An analysis of the discursive positions of women smokers: implications for practical interventions

## VAL GILLIES

There is now compelling evidence to link cigarette smoking with ill health and early death. It is estimated that approximately half of all regular cigarette smokers will eventually die from tobacco-related diseases (Doll *et al*. 1994). Women, it seems, are at particular risk of contracting a smoking-related illness. As well as the increased dangers of heart disease, lung cancer and emphysema, women smokers also face the additional hazards of cervical cancer, premature menopause and osteoporosis (Health Education Authority 1992). Regardless of these clearly documented health risks, and despite numerous public health campaigns, an estimated 26 per cent of women in the UK are, at present, regular smokers (Office of Population Censuses and Surveys 1994). Evidence also appears to suggest that fewer women than men successfully give up cigarette smoking (Stoto 1986).

Theories as to why smokers persist despite the negative consequences tend to centre on biological, social and cognitive explanations. Biological explanations focus on aspects of physical dependence that are associated with the chemical substances inhaled as cigarette smoke. In particular, nicotine is identified as a substance that activates the nervous system, increases the heart rate and generally stimulates or arouses (Sarafino 1990).

However, Jacobson (1981) questions the grounds for comparing the physical effects of nicotine to the physiological dependence associated with narcotic drugs such as opiates. Although initially smokers develop a tolerance to the effects of nicotine, there is not a steady increment in the number of cigarettes smoked over time. In addition, although many smokers experience withdrawal symptoms when they stop smoking, many, unlike opiate users, do not. Clearly, the biological explanation of physical addiction cannot alone account for the prevalence of cigarette smoking. Although relapse rates are high, many people successfully give up smoking for good. In 1979, the Surgeon General in the United States estimated that around 29 million people had given up smoking in the previous 15 years, and it was claimed that 95 per cent had achieved this without professional help (Sarafino 1990).

Social approaches to understanding smoking behaviour are based on the influence of psychosocial forces. For example, it is suggested that the most persuasive factors associated with the uptake of cigarette smoking include a high prevalence of smoking among family and friends, combined with encouragement in the form of peer pressure (Leventhal *et al.* 1985). Studies examining the demographic patterns of smoking indicate that socio-economic factors are strongly associated with cigarette consumption. Smoking has a clear inverse relationship to socio-economic status, while smoking cessation is positively correlated with high socio-economic status (Adler *et al.* 1994). In a qualitative analysis of the link between women smoking and disadvantage, Graham (1993) suggests that many working-class women use smoking to cope with the conflicting stresses and pressures that structure their everyday lives. According to Graham, smoking provides a way of carrying on with difficult and demanding lives.

Evidently, social and economic conditions exert a highly significant influence on smoking behaviour, but despite the explanatory power of these factors, most psychological theories of smoking focus on individual cognitions. Social cognition models (SCMs) are currently the most popular psychological theory used to explain and predict smoking behaviour. These models examine how individual beliefs, attitudes and perceptions of real-world situations result in a specific action, e.g. smoking. Social cognition theories, in the main, assume that individuals carry out detailed subjective assessments of the costs and benefits involved in actions such as cigarette smoking (Becker 1974; Ajzen and Fishbein 1991).

Although these models are commonly used as theoretical foundations for health promotion interventions, SCMs are based on several problematic assumptions which limit their practical applicability. First, SCMs are based on a conceptualization of the smoker as a rational, consistent individual whose smoking behaviour rests on a personal evaluation of the pros and cons involved. Discursive psychologists and feminists have challenged this construction of the rational unitary subject, arguing that people inhabit a number of contradictory discursive positions depending on social context (Potter and Wetherell 1987; Weedon 1987). Second, SCMs assume that variables determining smoking behaviour can be identified and applied to smokers in all manner of different social positions. However, as Graham (1994) has noted, gender (and class) specific factors influence both smoking behaviour and self-disclosure of smoking behaviour. Third, SCMs focus only on the effects of cognitive representations on behaviour, ignoring the practical, structural constraints that limit the extent of volitional control. The relevance to working-class women of SCMs and resulting interventions is debatable. Women in the unskilled manual socio-economic group are still around three times more likely to smoke than men in the professional group (OPCS 1994). Arguably, the individualistic premise of SCMs actively works against the interests of working-class women by obscuring mechanisms of oppression, and thereby impeding social change. The high smoking levels and low cessation rate suggest there is a need to develop a more focused approach that incorporates the real experience and meaning of cigarette smoking for working-class women.

## Discourse analysis: an alternative approach

Discourse analysis represents a move to transcend cognitive conceptions of behaviour and instead centres on the socially constructed nature of reality. Rather than treating verbal accounts of attitudes and beliefs and perceptions as expressions of stable cognitive structures, discourse analysis sees language as the primary site for negotiating meaning. In contrast to Graham's (1993) causal interpretation of smoking as a coping strategy, this study attempts to understand how, rather than why, working-class women continue to smoke (see also Gillies and Willig 1997). A conceptualization of discourse is utilized in order to examine the way in which subjects are positioned or 'contained' by the language they use to define, describe and explain everyday experiences of cigarette smoking. This positioning occurs both actively and passively, in that the subject can be agentic in choosing her constructs while also defined by the availability and accessibility of discourses. So the focus of this study is on exploring how women position themselves, and are positioned, within available discourses. It is suggested that these discursive constructions work to constrain as well as facilitate certain behaviours and actions, and as such the use of discourse is seen not only as accounting for cigarette smoking but as actively maintaining this behaviour in the future.

At this juncture it is relevant to situate this study within a particular stance in terms of the contrasting positions assumed by various discourse analytic approaches. A major debate within discursive psychology concerns the existence of an objective reality outside of human discourse. Postmodernist conceptions of discourse analysis assume an extreme relativist position, claiming that the perception of reality is constituted in and through discourse, and that the objective of any analysis is to decipher the means through which the discourse is constructed (Edwards *et al.* 1995). However, as Burman and Parker (1993: 167) point out, this approach proscribes the holding of any concrete position or interpretation over and above any other; thus 'theory floats disconnected from any political position', and very real phenomena such as social deprivation, disempowerment and even physical ill health are denied any tangible object status. Parker (1992) adopts a critical realist approach to discourse analysis and as such overcomes the troubling consequences of extreme relativism. This study examines accounts of cigarette smoking within this framework of discourse analysis in order to generate a more in-depth understanding of the multiple meanings and significance working-class women attach to the practice of cigarette smoking. It will be argued that the identification of these discursive constructions has important implications for current health promotion strategies.

## Method

The study is based on a series of semi-structured interviews conducted in the respondents' own homes. Each interview lasted for approximately one hour. Interviews were tape-recorded and transcribed in detail.

The study focused on four working-class women (all mothers), aged between 20 and 60 years, from an interrelated background, a loose network of friends living in North London. Social class was originally defined using the Registrar General's Classification of Occupations. However, a more discursively oriented, multidimensional interpretation of class is a more appropriate method for this kind of analysis. Skeggs (1997) outlines the interlinked nature of class and gender in the production of subjectivity, and determines class status on the basis of access to resources and legitimation. Using this definition, all four of the women smokers are clearly working class.

### Method of analysis

The aim of the analysis was to understand the ways in which respondents construct the activity of cigarette smoking. This was achieved by identifying the discursive meanings attached to smoking behaviour and identifying the discourses which informed the accounts of cigarette smoking. For this purpose Parker's (1992: 5) definition of a discourse as 'a system of statements which constructs an object' was utilized.

The analysis of the interview data broadly observed the following process. First, an attempt was made to identify any recurrent formations in linguistic constructions by reading and re-reading the transcripts. Then all references linked to smoking behaviour and cigarettes were taken out of the text and organized using relevant themes. Patterns were identified both in terms of the similarity in composition or content, and in terms of the dissimilarity or contrasting nature of what was being said. This was done by highlighting all relevant references and making notes in the margins.

The next stage of the analysis involved identifying the discursive meanings that construct the activity of cigarette smoking. As the analysis proceeded links and networks of meaning were established. This progressive analytic complexity led to the identification of specific discourses. In the last stage of the analysis particular discursive constructions were chosen and expanded upon using quotations from the text as linguistic evidence. Hypotheses were then formed concerning the functions and effects of the relevant constructions and discourses.

## Analysis

### Discursive constructions used to explain and justify smoking behaviour

#### Discourse of addiction

All four respondents referred to their smoking behaviour in terms of an 'addiction', or 'habit', thereby positioning themselves as dependent on the physiological effects of tobacco. Although a number of subsequently contradictory constructions were employed (see below), a discourse of addiction was predominantly drawn on to frame references to smoking as an activity. For example, Mary states:

**Extract 1**

... 'Cos really it's um dic it's um a sort of an addiction really I mean when it all boils down to it it is an addiction isn't it I mean you get the nicotine and that in your blood and that ...

Constructions of physiological addiction are drawn from a scientific discourse that employs notions of cause and effect and objective facts. Thus respondents attributed their 'addiction' or 'habit' to biological or chemical causes of dependence (i.e. nicotine). For example, in response to the question 'how important is smoking to you now' Sarah states:

**Extract 2**

... It's like it's a drug it's er addictive er I do enjoy it *sometimes* um [2] I suppose really it's become part of my life it's a habit really ...

I think if you haven't had a fag for a long time the first fag you have is like a stimulant it's um goes straight into the bloodstream and goes to the brain . . . I think it relaxes people um and I think then it just becomes a habit a habit forming er er thing really . . . It's just a habit it's just a just a *really nasty horrible* bad habit and I just don't think I can break out . . .

In this extract smoking behaviour is constructed in terms of a deep-rooted physiological dependence. Sarah provides an account of her cigarette smoking by stating that cigarettes are 'a drug', 'addictive' and 'part of her life'. She then describes the physical actions of the 'drug', before moving on to present herself and other smokers as subject to the addictive properties of cigarettes. Consequently, the most powerful effect of this construction is to provide a deterministic explanation that emphasizes the smoker's lack of control over her actions.

The use of such a scientific discourse legitimizes this rejection of agency. As part of a discourse of science, the physiological constructions in the form of biological and chemical determinants are presented as having the objective status of a scientific fact. Therefore, such constructions are difficult to challenge and serve to pre-empt any potential requests to give up smoking by emphasizing the physiological hurdles that would have to be overcome.

The use of a scientific discourse is also characterized by the respondents' objectifying or distancing themselves when referring to the physiological effects of cigarette smoking. When Sarah talks about the specific biological and chemical changes she maintains an impersonal stance, referring to 'the bloodstream' and 'the brain', as opposed to 'my bloodstream' and 'my brain'. On the one hand this has the effect of compounding the authenticity of the scientific discourse by impersonalizing the information and equating it with fact rather than opinion. On the other it also serves to distance and desensitize the physical and potentially damaging effects of cigarette smoking.

Jane also firmly locates herself within a discourse of addiction, stressing the physical nature of the dependency. When asked how important smoking is to her, she states:

### Extract 3

How how important is it oh gosh [2] that's difficult to say um [2] it's an addiction it's a physical addiction with me I do actually think and when I have tried to give it up I [2] it doesn't matter if somebody's smoking in front of me it doesn't increase my cravings I crave anyway

Questioning the importance of smoking to Jane implicitly requests an explanation of why cigarettes are important to her. Such an explanation would require Jane to accept the role of her own decision-making processes in her smoking behaviour. The concept that cigarettes can be more or less important encourages an account based on an evaluation of the pleasures of smoking, and this is not commensurate with the deterministic notions associated with constructions of physical addiction. Consequently, Jane pronounces the question 'difficult' and replaces the concept of importance with a concept of addiction. She also emphasizes the physical basis of the addiction by stressing the irrelevance of her social surroundings. She craves whether or not others around her are smoking. This suggests that constructions of social influence are available to her but not appropriated by her in this instance.

### Control and self-regulation

Accounts of self-control or self-discipline in relation to cigarette smoking clearly contrast with the previously identified discourse of addiction. However, three of the respondents made use of these constructions at some point in the interviews. For example, in contradiction to her evaluation of smoking as a physiological addiction (extract 1), previously Mary had stated:

### Extract 4

. . . If there's a place where you can't smoke it don't worry me it don't worry me . . . It don't I don't sort of get agitated and think oh I've got to go somewhere and find somewhere in the corner where I can have a cigarette it don't worry me at all that much . . .

In this extract, Mary stresses her ability to cope without cigarettes in certain situations. She uses this construction in particular when she refers to her relationships with non-smokers.

By presenting herself as restrained and in control she emphasizes the socially modified nature of her smoking behaviour. For example, she goes on to state:

### Extract 5

. . . If I go round to like Mike's friends they don't smoke and it don't worry me and I mean like when I used to go round my daughter's house she don't like me smoking and the same with Lisa when I've been up her flat like all day and that been up there for dinner that's not bothered me . . .

In this extract Mary justifies her status as a smoker by presenting her behaviour as responsible and sanctioned by social circumstances. She conveys an acknowledgement and an acceptance that non-smokers may disapprove and emphasizes her ability to abstain in appropriate situations.

Mary's construction of self-control contradicts her evaluation of smoking as an addiction. However, her positioning as a smoker with self-control appears to relate only to her ability to moderate her smoking behaviour, and so when she discusses her potential to give up she re-employs a discourse of addiction. In contrast, Karen's location of herself within a discourse of self-control extends to her ability to 'pack up' smoking. Having described her smoking behaviour as a physiological addiction, Karen focuses on her ability to abstain.

**Extract 6**

But I seem to be alright at the moment I think it's because I don't smoke as much as I [1] like I could I could just easily pack up

Karen also stressed her self-control in social situations:

**Extract 7**

. . . I mean the amount of times I've said no when people have offered me and I say no and they say *go on have one* but I go no it's alright (laughs) yeah so I'd say you know I'm not too bad really 'cos some people just smoke for the sake of it I try and just smoke when I want one

By emphasizing the number of times she has said 'no' she positions herself as having will power and clear control over her actions. Attention is drawn to the fact that she often declines to smoke even in the face of strong social pressure. This explicitly signifies restraint and self-discipline, and also implicitly reinforces the assurance that, if she wanted to, she could stop smoking at any time. In stating that she smokes only when she wants one she is claiming free will and choice, which is associated with the inherently moral concept of individual responsibility for health. So by the acceptance of personal responsibility and emphasizing self-control and restraint a sense is conveyed that she is morally accountable and conscientious.

*Agency*
The apparently opposing positions of 'addiction' and 'self-control' assumed by the respondents indicate the variable ways in which agency can be understood. These contradictory constructions are both associated with issues of accountability and control over behaviour, and as such they highlight the dilemmatic aspects of these concepts.

Billig *et al.* (1988) point to a common tension in the attribution of agency as a result of an inevitable contention between the conflicting demands of individual freedom and physical necessity. These antithetical ideologies present individuals as both agents with free choice and objects determined by bodily materialism. As a result, individuals struggle with the demands of perceiving themselves as being simultaneously free and unfree.

The dilemmatic nature of agency in terms of cigarette smoking was specific-ally addressed in several of the interviews. For example, Sarah positions her actions as being determined when she describes her smoking behaviour in terms of an addiction. Lack of free will is also implied by her subsequent suggestion that tobacco should be banned for people's own good. Never-theless, when cigarette smoking is framed in terms of being a choice, Sarah moves to a position that emphasizes her free will.

### Extract 8

V: So if they did that [banned tobacco] that would in a way be removing your *choice* to smoke

S: Yes it is but er yeah it is actually isn't it but um if they said they were thinking about it maybe people would think twice there's so many people who don't smoke now actually it's a gradual brain washing thing you know

V: Yeah

S: Um your choice to smoke I think it's a good they've banned it on buses trains tubes er and some public places that's pretty good I that's another thing about what you said it's a choice as to whether you smoke or not really

V: Is that how you feel do you feel like you're actually making a choice?

S: Yeah I am

V: You are

S: Yeah I'm making a choice to smoke even though I've got that fighting guilt because I know it's wrong it's making it's giving me cancer but I still do it (laughs)

The suggestion that smoking is a choice was clearly located within a framework of free will and individual choice, and Sarah accordingly adapts her position to incorporate these concepts. Her claim that the threat of a tobacco ban would make people 'think twice' is clearly based on the pre-mise that smokers are capable of deciding whether to smoke or not, although her reference to a 'gradual brainwashing thing' continues to imply a lack of control.

The theme of responsibility and control over behaviour is emphasized by Sarah's approval of non-smoking buses and trains. If people are choosing whether to smoke then irresponsible smoking behaviour needs to be con-tained. When the issue is personalized Sarah acknowledges that she actively chooses to smoke. So her acceptance of a discourse of free will requires her to accept responsibility as a smoker rather than as an 'addict'. Sarah's description of her free will is qualified by her statement that she is 'fighting guilt' and knows 'it's wrong'. These moral implications are addressed as part of her construction of choice and free will, because if she chooses to smoke then she is responsible for the consequences.

## Constructions of acceptable and unacceptable smoking

Respondents commonly evaluated smoking behaviour in moral terms by positioning themselves as respectable smokers, while denouncing other 'types' of smokers. For example, Karen distinguishes between good and bad smokers and then goes on to justify her own smoking behaviour. Having recently switched from smoking manufactured cigarettes to smoking roll-ups, she projects the negative consequences of smoking on to smokers of manufactured cigarettes.

### Extract 9

*K:* Well the smoke from cigarette is different from the smoke from roll ups isn't it

*V:* Mmh

*K:* You know like the smoke from a cigarette is much worse

*V:* Is it?

*K:* Oh yeah ten times worse I mean I was waiting for a bus and there was this women smoking a cigarette and it made me feel really ill

Karen constructs cigarette smoke as noxious in comparison to the smoke from roll-ups and stresses how offensive and annoying it is to other people. So by focusing on a major disadvantage of manufactured cigarettes (the smoke), she vindicates her own type of smoking. She is also able to position herself as a victim of passive smoking rather than a perpetrator.

Mary also constructs smoking behaviour in terms of acceptable and unacceptable smokers. In the following extract, she outlines an appropriate code of behaviour for smokers.

### Extract 10

. . . If you're in company with other people who don't smoke you don't bother you see because you're being anti-social well you are aren't you I mean if you're in a room with people that don't smoke I mean you shouldn't really I mean I dare say some people would but I wouldn't myself do it and that

By conveying the principle that it is not acceptable to smoke when others around you are non-smokers, Mary positions herself as a moral smoker who is sensitive to the rights of other individuals. Her acknowledgement that 'some people would' emphasizes the controlled and socially responsible nature of her behaviour by contrasting it with the unrestrained, inconsiderate actions that others engage in.

### Defusing health hazards

The harmful consequences associated with cigarette smoking were addressed in all four interviews. In discussing the risks and also in giving general accounts of smoking behaviour, respondents used various constructions in order to minimize or deny the health risks associated with cigarette smoking.

For instance, Mary plays down her personal risk by emphasizing the major risks taken by other smokers.

### Extract 11

V: Do you ever worry about yourself the sort of health thing?

M: Well I do sort of sometimes I think well I should pack it up 'cos um well I say well a neighbour of mine over the road Daisy she died she was a very heavy smoker smoked cigarettes a *very very* heavy smoker and she died last year mind you she had cancer and 'cos she never ever went to the doctors she left it till the last minute you know and she never had check ups or anything like that um I do go for um I do go regular for check-ups you know all breast check-ups and smear test and everything like that . . .

In this extract, Mary's acknowledgement of the health hazard is conveyed by her admission that she should 'pack it up'. However, this is soon followed by an interpretation that excludes Mary from the major risks. Having portrayed her neighbour, Daisy, as a victim of cigarette smoking, she proceeds to account for this by emphasizing Daisy's extreme status as a *'very very* heavy smoker'. The specific circumstances leading to Daisy's death are also depicted as unusual. Unlike Mary, she never went to the doctor for check-ups and avoided reporting her illness until the last minute. The significance of this contrast is repeated further on in the interview.

### Extract 12

. . . The woman over the road she smoked for years and she'd been having pains and losing weight and she never ever did anything about it she probably could have been saved but she was terrified of doctors and hospitals but I'm not a person like that I'm not terrified of doctors you know if I think anything's amiss you know I go round there I don't pester the doctors but if I thought suddenly I started losing weight I'd think to myself right there's something wrong

In this context, the example of Mary's neighbour is used specifically to address the risk of contracting cancer. Again the contributing character-istics are emphasized, i.e. Daisy had smoked for years and ignored the pains and weight loss because she was afraid of doctors. Mary, on the other hand, stresses how she is alert and wary, almost to the point of pestering the doctors. Mary's claim that Daisy probably could have been saved also indicates an optimism about individual control over health. Consequently, health concerns are further defused by a faith in medical attention to detect and cure any signs of cancer.

Sarah also positions herself as sceptical towards claims about the health hazards of smoking, despite expressing concern about the effects of smoke on her daughter. She minimized the basis for concern by questioning the factual basis of passive smoking and focusing on the unreliable and incon-sistent history of medical advice.

**Extract 13**

V: So what would convince you then?

S: What would convince me good visible docu documented evidence

V: What do you mean by documented?

S: You know something that's really been um thought out 'cos you're never *never* certain because last year they said butter gave you cancer

V: Mmh

S: This year they're saying it's good to have a little bit of butter but not so much in moderation so really it would have to be some form some some kind of evidence that would be um that's it now you've said it that's the truth and what [unclear] five years later they're not going to say sorry we were wrong

Sarah's appeal for 'good visible documented evidence' suggests that current information is not convincing. Evidence would have to be certain and irrefut-able in order for Sarah to accept that her cigarette smoke is detrimental. However, the level of certainty she demands ensures there will always be room for doubt. Sarah is claiming that she would have to be 100 per cent certain that scientists and doctors will not suddenly discover that they were mistaken. By suggesting that evidence will never be certain enough, Sarah is able to continue denying or minimizing the health effects of cigarettes.

Sarah also commonly relied on extreme case formulations (Pomerantz 1986) to defuse the threat of health risks, in that she often employed explanations and accounts that invoked exaggerated or extreme instances. According to Pomerantz, presenting an exaggerated or overstated example of a particular evaluative dimension can provide an effective justification for maintaining a specific position. In Sarah's case, she employs extreme case formulations both to position herself as safe and to warrant her smoking behaviour in the face of the health risks.

### Extract 14

... Anything that you put into your body anything apart from like [1] well what's fresh air fresh air's full of pollution (laughs) er you know everything's bad for you to a to a er er extent but those things like alcohol cigarettes taking drugs popping pills even being even coming down to contraception are not good for you in the long run are going to upset the whole workings of your body or do something

From a perspective that presents everything as potentially harmful, cigarette smoking becomes just another danger associated with modern day life. When pollution in the air is compared to cigarette smoke the latter becomes less threatening. Sarah also draws on an interesting construction of 'the body' as a delicately balanced mechanism not designed to cope with modern society. This suggests there was a time when the body was in harmony with its surroundings and not upset by pollution, drugs and contraception. This conception of contemporary life as unnatural again provides a warrant for smoking behaviour. Smoking may be harmful and unhealthy but so is modern life.

By contrast, Jane is categorical in her acceptance of the health hazards associated with smoking. Health risks are interpreted by Jane as further evidence that she is a victim of the addictive qualities of cigarette smoking. Jane diminishes the significance of smoking-related diseases by presenting them as an unavoidable consequence of her addiction. As an addict, she is helpless and out of control, and so focusing on the harmful consequences of smoking serves no useful purpose. In the following extract, Jane describes how doctors have attempted to persuade her to give up.

### Extract 15

*J:* So you sort of like say yeah yeah well you know it's really bad for your health you know yeah yeah but those those arguments don't wash you know

*V:* Mmh

*J:* It's you know you've heard it all before you know

To Jane, the health 'arguments' are hackneyed and ineffectual because they are based on a premise that the decision to smoke is rational, rather than on an acceptance that smoking behaviour is physiologically determined. Jane stresses that the health risks can have no influence over her behaviour, as she is already aware of the dangers. She has 'heard it all before' and doctors 'reading the riot act' cannot make her feel responsible for a behaviour which she has no control over. By positioning herself as physiologically determined and unable to exert conscious control, she effectively defuses the health hazards associated with smoking.

## Medicinalization of smoking

Respondents commonly referred to constructions of cigarettes as palliative or medicinal. Smoking was generally portrayed as a relaxing, calming activity, and when relating particularly stressful situations respondents often attributed therapeutic properties to cigarettes. For example, in extract 16 Mary describes the difficult period she experienced after the birth of her first baby.

### Extract 16

I had her and that of course she used to scream and cry and grizzle and that *and oh my god* you think you're going mad *you literally feel* you know when people say to you they could kill someone well that's the state you get in you get so no you know you get in a state and you think to yourself you must calm down calm yourself down have a cup of tea and a cigarette calms calms you down you know

Implicit in this extract is the serious nature of Mary's 'state'. She emphasizes how she felt dangerously out of control and close to breakdown. The soothing effect of cigarettes is described as a vital remedy, averting mental breakdown and helping to preserve stability under extremely stressful conditions.

Cigarettes were also described in terms of their prophylactic properties, particularly with regard to preventing stress. In the following extract Mary describes her smoking behaviour during a particularly stressful period when her husband was in hospital and her mother-in-law was staying with her.

### Extract 17

M: 'Cos when Mike was came out he was improving you know and she went home I went back to normal like you know but we had two very traumatic weeks like you know I was sort of you know every bloody half hour I think I was lighting up a fag you know and um

V: So that helped the stress

J: Well I think if I hadn't have done if I hadn't have done Val I think I would have exploded and had a terrible row and caused a lot of um bad feeling and um all in the family and that you know it it calms me down you know

In this situation Mary describes how she used cigarettes as an antidote to stress. By smoking Mary repressed unwanted emotions and avoided the serious consequences of an emotional 'explosion'.

Sarah also referred to cigarette smoking in terms of the therapeutic benefits. Extract 18 follows on from Sarah's description of her boyfriend's attitude to her smoking.

**Extract 18**

V: So he does moan at you sometimes for smoking
S: Yeah but the other night when I got attacked and my handbag nearly got nicked he said go and have one (laughs) so I think him being an ex-smoker he realizes the comfort
V: Right yeah so
S: See he
V: So does he ever smoke
S: He he the last time I remember him smoking was when his Nan and Dad died
V: Right
S: Which I understand completely I think he understands under due due stress that it's something you do turn to so

Sarah's admission that her boyfriend generally disapproves of smoking conveys the principle that extenuating circumstances warrant a turn to cigarettes. The fact that he gave his permission, and even encouraged her to smoke, is presented as evidence of the therapeutic function of smoking. As an ex-smoker, Sarah's boyfriend understands the soothing, healing 'comfort' that is generated by smoking a cigarette. The medicinal value of cigarette smoking is further emphasized by the way that an ex-smoker still turns to cigarettes in times of stress. The fact that 'due stress' provides a justification for even non-smokers to relapse reinforces the suggestion that cigarettes play an important role in stress management.

**Discussion**

This analysis has identified various discursive constructions used by working-class women to explain and justify smoking behaviour. As such, it provides an insight into the meaning and significance of cigarette smoking to the respondents, and may promote a greater understanding of why individuals engage in a behaviour which is so obviously detrimental to health.

It is argued that the discourses and discursive constructions that have been explored in this analysis shape how these women behave and experience the world. Consequently, there is a need for this analysis to be located within a cultural context. The fact that all four respondents drew on a discourse of addiction undoubtedly reflects the strength and prevalence of this construction in society. The medical establishment in particular appears to locate the incidence of cigarette smoking within a disease model, perceiving it as a physical problem in need of treatment. For example, the British Medical Association's *Complete Family Health Encyclopaedia* (1990) states the following in a section on 'Health and medicine today': 'Both alcohol and nicotine are addictive drugs; people who begin smoking or drinking socially often find themselves, several years later, unable to give up the habit.' The assumption that individuals can become dependent on cigarettes or tobacco is often likened to opiate addiction and accordingly presented as one end of a continuum of severity of consequences. For instance, Dr Chris Steel, a popular television doctor presented as a specialist in smoking cessation, was quoted in the *Independent on Sunday* (4 June 1995) as claiming that addiction to nicotine is ten times more powerful than addiction to heroin. This constitutes a powerfully deterministic view and leaves little room for encouraging those attempting to give up.

Dominant theories of smoking behaviour associated with medical and psychological institutions inform the disciplines and practices of health promotion and health education. Consequently, a discourse of addiction can be identified as running through various public health campaigns aimed at discouraging smoking. For instance, a leaflet from the Health Education Authority (1994) aimed specifically at pregnant women states the following under the heading 'Expect to feel rough': 'Nicotine in cigarettes is addictive. If you were a heavy smoker your body will have to get use to managing without.'

The prevalence of a discourse of addiction among the respondents can also be related to gender issues. In discussing attributions of smoking behaviour, Jacobson (1981) claims that women are more likely to perceive themselves as being addicted. According to Jacobson, the role of the 'helpless addict' begins early on in life and is associated with traditional sex roles. As Jacobson (1981) notes, young men characteristically deny attributions of nicotine addiction and tend to emphasize their ability to give up at any time. Notions of dependency, on the other hand, are predominantly associated with women. This may provide something of an insight into why levels of smoking cessation are significantly lower for women than for men.

This dominant construction of cigarette smoking as a physiological addiction is, in many respects, disempowering and negative. As Peele (1990) points out, the belief that smoking is caused by an addiction evokes a frightening world view that portrays it as hopeless for people to try to control their own lives or habits. Peele is also concerned that such concepts of addiction are presented as if they were based on scientific fact, when in contrast evidence points more towards the role of personal outlook and social setting.

In terms of the implications for health promotion strategies, it can be argued that a discourse of addiction is counterproductive when used to explain and account for smoking behaviour. The more convinced an individual is of her addiction the less likely she is to attempt to give up. A study by Eiser (1984) suggests that self-attributions of addiction actually reduce a smoker's ability to give up. Notions of addiction can only foster and encourage negative self-fulfilling prophecies, and this is clearly supported by the positionings identified in the analysis. Respondents consistently used a discourse of addiction to account for why they continued to smoke and to explain why they were unable to give up. The fact that constructions of self-control were also drawn on by respondents is encouraging in terms of refuting negative, fatalistic conceptions of smoking behaviour. It indicates that respondents had access to more empowering and less passive constructions of their cigarette smoking. Nevertheless, an overemphasis on restraint can also be counterproductive, and the representations of self-control in society and culture can be traced back to a political agenda, especially in terms of health. Concepts of self-control and restraint are generally encouraged as positive and desirable attributes within society. They are associated with will power, resolution and strength of character, while a lack of self-control is regarded as weak, incapable and self-indulgent. The notion of self-control is also closely linked to ideas of social and individual responsibility. However, an ideology that promotes concepts of personal responsibility for health and individual choice frequently ignores the complex social and economic factors that are known to be strong determinants of overall health status (Townsend *et al.* 1988).

Replacing a discourse of addiction with a construction of self control is not necessarily a positive step, in that it can foster self blaming and guilt and thereby actively impede health promotion objectives. As Rodmell and Watt (1987) argue, attempts to alter entrenched patterns of behaviour will be ineffectual without considerable changes in social conditions. Therefore, too much emphasis on self-control and personal choice can only result in a negative backlash when a failure to give up smoking results in feelings of inadequacy or even resentment and anger. Health promotion campaigns aimed at encouraging smokers to give up need to focus on individual behaviour and self-control in order to empower people to take control of their health. However, such interventions must also recognize that the structural determinants of health are often outside an individual's control and need to be confronted at a political level.

The contradictory themes of addiction (physical determinism) and self-control (individual freedom) uncovered in the interviews deal specifically with accountability for behaviour. Thus, the dilemmatic nature of determining agency in terms of cigarette smoking clearly reflects the wider opposition between freedom and physical necessity. As Billig *et al.* (1988: 97) note, 'health is becoming less a passive backdrop to life and more an aspect to be worked upon and directed.' Consequently, the freedom to remain healthy becomes dependent on following a number of rules that dictate how life must be lived.

In terms of further implications for health promotion strategies, the fact that respondents commonly outlined acceptable and unacceptable constructions of cigarette smoking in order to vindicate their own smoking behaviour is of note. Anti-smoking campaigns regularly circulate morally loaded messages focusing on the detrimental effects of cigarettes on non-smokers. Women in particular tend to be targeted in such a way. The respondents' portrayal of 'good' and 'bad' smokers can be interpreted in terms of countering these potential moral objections. By joining in with a vilification of irresponsible smokers the respondents were able to compare themselves favourably with constructions of immoral smokers. In other words, they were not prepared to identify with a portrayal of all smokers as selfish and lacking in social conscience.

As Jacobson (1981) points out, health education campaigns aimed at women invariably focus on their roles as wives and mothers. Jacobson cites in particular the Health Education Council's 'Smoking in Pregnancy Campaign' which during the 1970s used slogans such as 'Is it fair to force your baby to smoke cigarettes?' Although less dramatic, more recent attempts to dissuade women from smoking take a similar approach. A leaflet issued by the Health Education Authority in 1994 used TV presenter Ann Diamond as a figurehead. The leaflet was entitled 'Give your baby a head start', and stated: 'If there was a simple way of giving your baby the biggest chance of a healthy start in life, wouldn't you take it? Of course you would.' Apart from its patronizing tone, this leaflet is notable in that it fails to mention what the benefits of stopping would be for the mother. As Jacobson states, the health education messages directed at women generally depend on generating guilt and anxiety. The underlying assumption is that a women would be more likely to modify her behaviour for the sake of others.

Gender issues may also be prominent in the respondents' medicinalization of cigarette smoking. The fact that cigarettes were constructed as medicinal aids for controlling moods and emotions reflects the wider pressures on women to repress unacceptable feelings. Aggressive or angry reactions from women are generally disapproved of and pathologized. So, for example, Mary's aggressive 'state' (Extract 16) is presented as an aberrant condition in need of relieving.

Although the practical implications of this study for health promotion strategies have been mentioned, it is nevertheless important to question the ethical basis for changing smoking behaviour. From a discourse analytic perspective, discursive positions structure subjectivity and identity, and consequently health promotion objectives could be interpreted as an attempt to 'govern the soul' (Rose 1989). Striving to control how an individual experiences subjectivity is a questionable route to improving health. Furthermore, the advantages of smoking cessation for working-class women are not necessarily clear cut. Although the health risks cannot be disputed, it could be argued that they are offset by the less obvious benefits of smoking to working-class women. The use of cigarettes as a coping strategy is a commonly documented feature of women's smoking. Graham (1994) notes how cigarette smoking among young mothers is often central to the management of anger and the avoidance of physical abuse.

However, both these concerns are based on a particular conception of health promotion as goal based and necessarily encouraging conformity. Health promotion work could be viewed as empowering if its objectives were to increase the number of positive, accessible positionings available to working-class women. For example, it is suggested that discourses constructing a more positive conception of the body could be promoted. Rather than viewing the body as a dominant, controlling force, as in a discourse of addiction, or as a separate entity in need of regulation and repression, as in a construction of self-control, a more affirmative construction would emphasize pleasure, strength and vitality. As Ettorre (1994) notes about women and substance use, the experience of pleasure associated with the use of drugs needs to be replaced instead of denied. Thus strategies aimed at encouraging cessation could include free or cheap access to gyms, aerobics classes or meditation courses, in order to promote alternative forms of physical enjoyment.

The claim that cigarettes may represent a positive resource for working-class women highlights the need for health promotion efforts to be grounded in structural issues. It is vitally important that the basis of working-class women's oppression is addressed. As Ettorre (1994) suggests, collective frameworks are important in supporting the development of social agency and positive self-definition. If working-class women, as a specific community, can address the issues associated with cigarette smoking, then self-help strategies can be grounded in social change, and the more oppressive ideologies associated with substance use can be replaced with more positive self-affirming practices.

## References

Adler N. E., Boyce, T., Chesney, M. A., Cohen, S., Folkman, S., Kahn, R. and Syme, S. L. (1994) Socio-economic status and health: the challenge of the gradient, *American Psychologist*, 49(1): 15–24.

Ajzen, I. and Fishbein, M. (1991) The theory of planned behaviour, *Organisational Behaviour and Human Decision Processes*, 50: 179–211.

Becker, M. H. (1974) The health belief model and personal health behaviour, *Health Education Monographs*, 2: 324–598.

Billig, M. (1987) *Arguing and Thinking: A Rhetorical Approach to Social Psychology*. Cambridge: Cambridge University Press.

Billig, M., Condor, S., Edwards, D., Gane, M., Middleton, D. and Radley, A. (1988) *Ideological Dilemmas: A Social Psychology of Everyday Thinking*. London: Sage.

British Medical Association (1990) *Complete Family Health Encyclopaedia*. London: Dorling Kindersley.

Burman, E. and Parker, I. (1993) Against discursive imperialism, empiricism and constructionism: thirty-two problems with discourse analysis. In E. Burman and I. Parker (eds) *Discourse Analytic Research*. London: Routledge.

Chesney, M. (1991) Women, stress and smoking. In M. Frankenhaeuser, U. Lundberg and M. Chesney (eds) *Women, Work and Health*. New York: Plenum Press.

Doll, R., Peto, R., Wheatley, K., Gray, R. and Sutherland, I. (1994) Mortality in relation to smoking: 40 years' observations on male british doctors, *British Medical Journal*, 309: 889–90.

Edwards, D., Ashmore, M. and Potter, J. (1995) Death and furniture: the rhetoric, politics and theology of bottom line arguments against relativism, *History of the Human Sciences*, 8: 25–49.

Eiser, J. R. (1984) Addiction as attribution: cognitive processes in giving up smoking. In J. R. Eiser (ed.) *Social Psychology and Behaviour Medicine*. Chichester: Wiley.

Ettorre, E. (1994) Substance use and women's health. In S. Wilkinson and C. Kitzinger (eds) *Women and Health: Feminist Perspectives*. London: Taylor and Francis.

Gillies, V. and Willig, C. (1997) 'You get the nicotine and that in your blood': constructions of addiction and control in women's accounts of cigarette smoking, *Journal of Community and Applied Social Psychology*, 7: 285–301.

Graham, H. (1994) Surviving by smoking. In S. Wilkinson and C. Kitzinger (eds) *Women and Health: Feminist Perspectives*. London: Taylor and Francis.

Graham, H. (1993) *When Life's a Drag: Women, Smoking and Disadvantage*. London: HMSO.

Health Education Authority (1992) *The Smoking Epidemic: A Manifesto for Action in England*. London: HEA.

Health Education Authority (1993) *Smoking and Pregnancy*. London: HEA.

Jacobson, J. (1981) *The Ladykillers: Why Smoking Is a Feminist Issue*. London: Pluto Press.

Kumar, R. (1976) Is nicotine important in tobacco smoking?, *Clinical Pharmacology and Therapeutics*, 21(5): 871–8.

Leventhal, H., Prohaska, T. and Hirschman, R. (1985) Preventive health behaviour across the life span. In J. Rosen and L. Solomon (eds) *Prevention in Health Psychology*. Hanover, NH: New England University Press.

Office of Population Censuses and Surveys (1994) *General Household Survey*. London: HMSO.

Parker, I. (1992) *Discourse Dynamics: Critical Analysis for Social and Individual Psychology*. London: Routledge.

Peele, S. (1990) Behaviour in a vacuum: social psychological theories of addiction that deny the social and psychological meanings of behaviour, *Journal of Mind and Behaviour*, 11(3/4): 513–29.

Pomerantz, A. (1986) Extreme case formulations: a new way of legitimating claims. In G. Button, P. Drew and J. Heritage (eds) *Human Studies* (Interaction and language use special issue), 9: 219–30.

Potter, J. and Wetherell, M. (1987) *Discourse and Social Psychology: Beyond Attitudes and Behaviour*. London: Sage.

Rodmell, S. and Watt, A. (1987) Community involvement in health promotion: progress or panacea?, *Health Promotion*, 2(4): 359–68.

Rose, N. (1989) *Governing the Soul*. London: Routledge.

Sarafino, E. P. (1990) *Health Psychology*. Singapore: Wiley.

Skeggs, B. (1997) *Formations of Class and Gender*. London: Sage.

Stoto, M. A. (1986) Changes in adult smoking behaviour in the United States 1953–1983, *Journal of Occupational Medicine*, 28: 360–4.

Townsend, P., Davidson, N. and Whitehead, M. (1988) *Inequalities in Health*. Harmondsworth: Penguin.

Weedon, C. (1987) *Feminist Practice and Poststructuralist Theory*. Oxford: Blackwell.

# 5 Deconstructing and reconstructing: producing a reading on 'human reproductive technologies'

## JOAN PUJOL

Linguistic philosophy has moved traditional methodological issues away from the idealistic experimental paradigm. *The Linguistic Turn* (Rorty 1967) was a turning point in the relevance given to language in social theory. The book contained a selection of texts in what was seen at the time as a revolutionary movement in philosophy: 'the purpose of the present volume is to provide materials for reflection on the most recent philosophical revolution, that of linguistic philosophy' (Rorty 1967: 3). The linguistic philosophical movement and the hermeneutic tradition have had an important influence in social psychology that can be exemplified, in the British context, through alternative perspectives such as discourse (Potter and Wetherell 1987; Parker 1992), rhetoric (Billig 1987), Q-methodology (Brown 1980; Stainton-Rogers 1995) or textuality (Curt 1994). The central role that language has in the theories and methods currently being developed in social sciences illustrates the impact and influence of 'the linguistic turn'. Everyday language and the construction of meaning are central topics in present social research. Nuclear concepts such as identity, society, person or power have been redefined using language and discourse as constitutive elements. The central role textual perspectives give to language has transformed Wittgenstein's quote: 'the limits of my language are the limits of my world' (Wittgenstein 1921: §5.6).[1] The danger of linguistic and hermeneutic perspectives, as Bhaskar argues, is to analyse statements about 'being' in terms of 'our knowledge about being' (Bhaskar 1975: 13); in other words, to assume that it is possible to reduce questions of ontology (the nature of the world) to epistemological issues (the knowledge of the world). The analytic and theoretical rejection of entities outside language constitutes the most controversial issue of textual perspectives.

The issue of 'intention of the text' will be used to explore and illustrate some of the methodological issues at stake.[2] As language does not merely 'describe' the world but 'acts' in the world, intentionality becomes a central concept, although the distinction between the 'text' and the 'intention of the text' becomes problematic. Where the participants' orientation is to be considered, the agents in interaction are transformed into 'intentional speakers' and 'understanding listeners', leading to a number of problematic implications (Harris 1988). First, analysis overlooks the network of textual and contextual connections in which the speaker is immersed. Participants would have to be mutually aware of other people's intentions and their discursive actions depend on such understanding. The 'intention of the text' opens the door to an entity outside the immediate textual interaction. A similar problem arises when the 'intention' is located in the social realm. In order to maintain the 'textual' nature of the world it is necessary to postulate that the entity outside interaction is also textual, thus conceptualizing both people's intentions (i.e. in terms of subjectivity) and societal purposes (i.e. power) as discursive. Bhaskar's critical realism offers a way out by distinguishing between the 'epistemological' and 'ontological' realm. While acknowledging the epistemological impossibility of arriving at 'the reality behind manifestation', it affirms its necessary existence. Nevertheless, Derrida, in his criticisms of Husserl's phenomenology (Derrida 1973) and Austin's speech-act theory (Derrida 1977) has exposed the problems arising from such a strategy. The core of the argument is based on the difficulty of establishing any correspondence between 'intention' and 'text' (or 'sense' and 'speech') once the distance between the two concepts has been affirmed. Postulating some form of experience or intention acting as a substratum underlying and giving meaning to speech opens up a gap between 'the experience' and 'what is said about the experience'. The perceptual experience (e.g. the colour white) becomes relatively independent of its expressive function (e.g. 'this is white'), construing the relationship between the experiential (or intentional) and the expressive as intrinsically problematic (Derrida 1973: 115–21).

The problematic nature of the relationship between 'text' and 'reality' can also be applied to the 'researcher' and the 'text'; in other words, the problem of how to ground the researcher's access to the 'meanings' of the text. Our answer will follow Gadamer's perspective. He argues, contrary to previous hermeneutic perspectives, against the possibility of overcoming such distance (Gadamer 1960). Schleiermacher, for example, considered that because author and reader share a common language, an empathetic understanding uncovering the subjectivity of the author was possible. To postulate the existence of an intuitive shared understanding which grounds interpretation implies that the analysis has to rely on the competence of the analyst in 'connecting' with participants' understandings, and this is precisely what needs to be uncovered by this same analysis. By contrast, influenced by Heidegger, Gadamer considers that the researcher cannot escape from the limitations imposed by being-in-the-world, by pertaining to a specific temporal and spatial context. Instead of grounding interpretation on a romantic reading of the text based on what is shared between reader and text, he considers that interpretation is possible precisely because the reader is located in a particular position. Understanding emerges from the prejudices and preconceptions of the reader and not despite them. The horizon of the interpreter is an essential component in the understanding of the horizon of the text and, therefore, interpretation is not a process of revealing the text but of fusion with the text. It is precisely by acknowledging the distance from the 'other' that meaning is produced.

Every encounter with tradition that takes place within historical consciousness involves the experience of a tension between the text and the present. The hermeneutic task consists not in covering up this tension by attempting a naive assimilation of the two, but in consciously bringing it out. This is why it is part of the hermeneutic approach to project a historical horizon of the past that is different from the horizon of the present (Gadamer 1960: 306).

From this perspective, interpretation emerges from the inevitable distance between traditions. Instead of assimilation of one tradition by another, hermeneutics suggests interpretation as a process of exploration and recognition of the space between perspectives. One of the methodological implications of such an assumption is the impossibility of uncovering 'the author' or the 'reality' behind a text. Therefore, interpretation is not about 'uncovering what is behind' but 'constructing it' through the interaction between text and reader. In an interview with Richard Kearney, Derrida describes the relationship between reader and text in the following terms:

> Deconstruction gives pleasure in that it gives desire. To deconstruct a text is to disclose how it functions as desire, as a search for presence and fulfilment which is interminably deferred. One cannot read without opening oneself to the desire of language, to the search for that which remains absent and other than oneself. Without a certain love for the text, no reading would be possible. In every reading there is a

corps-à-corps between reader and text, an incorporation of the reader's desire into the desire of the text. Here is pleasure, the very opposite of that arid intellectualism of which deconstruction has so often been accused.

(Kearney 1984: 126)

This approach emphasizes 'absence' instead of 'presence', 'difference' instead of 'identity'. These ideas suggest an understanding of discursive research in terms not of 'describing' but of 'construing' participants' understandings by exploring the distance between researcher and researched. At the same time, the relationship with the object of research is not avoided but encouraged as a search for an impossible fusion. The play between strangeness and familiarity constitutes the basis for interpretation. To conceptualize research not as the 'uncovering of hidden meanings' but as an 'active construction' emerging from the relationship between researcher and researched opens up a space for reconsidering the concepts of 'application' and 'interpretation'. The concept of 'application' assumes an understanding (or a better understanding) that grounds, or suggests, some form of 'action' in the world. One applies some 'knowledge', produced from a disciplinary area, to a certain phenomenon. The term 'applied social psychology' assumes that the discipline 'social psychology' can produce distinctive knowledge potentially useful in different contexts. The concept of 'application' is important for perspectives which identify a need to produce knowledge of 'reality' to ground social action, such as critical realism.

Bhaskar (1975) links the emancipatory function of social sciences with the knowledge of the structures giving shape to social life. Nevertheless, it is difficult to reduce the complexities of social reality to the degree of specialization and specificity characteristic of disciplinary knowledge. The traditional common answer has been to analyse the problem from an interdisciplinary perspective using as many perspectives as possible, with each discipline offering its unique practical knowledge. Because of the lack of a common language between disciplines and the proliferation of disciplinary fields, this approach has also been questioned.

Transdisciplinarity[3] focuses on the issue that needs to be addressed instead of paying attention to the discipline, to the knowledge that needs to be used. Moving from 'discipline' to 'phenomenon', from 'knowledge' to 'action', implies an emphasis on 'intervention' over 'application'. The emphasis is on the action taken and the knowledge emerging from such action, instead of the 'understanding' and the action derived from such understanding. Answers become local, deriving not from general disciplinary knowledge but from specific relationships with the phenomenon. To consider research as an 'intervention' instead of a form of knowledge production dissolves the dichotomy between 'theory' and 'application'. Social research becomes an active creation of understandings in order to produce a certain effect, a certain action. Interpretive research moves from 'what is said in the text' to 'what can be said from the text' (Ricoeur 1981: 93). While traditionalism generates readings that reproduce and legitimize the present social order, critical analysis aims to engender readings which challenge widespread beliefs (Ricoeur 1981: 112). The text does not function as a mirror of societal discourses but as a tool to create a possible world where action can be projected. The distinction between 'hermeneutics of meaning' and 'hermeneutics of suspicion' (Ricoeur 1981) is of relevance. According to Ricoeur, interpretation should not become a tool to restore certain meanings; instead it should use the text to demystify and question the meanings incrusted in the tradition of the reader. Interpretation is not the end but the beginning of a process of questioning, challenging and demystification. From this perspective, research becomes an intervention, and the researcher produces not merely a certain understanding of the world but an action on it.

To summarize, I have argued for social research within a post-empiricist paradigm emphasizing the importance of 'meaning construction' instead of the 'uncovering of hidden meanings'. From this perspective, application, the use of expert knowledge in practical contexts, gives way to 'intervention', getting involved with the problem and gaining knowledge through this involvement. The uneasy relationship between researcher and object of research produces a productive assemblage combining textual and material elements.

In the following section a research study partly exemplifying the principles outlined above is presented. It draws on the division between 'reader' (researcher), 'text' (data) and 'reading' (results). This structure allows us to explore the perspective of the researcher on the social practices analysed, the procedure to construct a certain text and the productive tension between reader and text.

## The reader's perspective on human reproductive technologies

My interest in producing a reading in the area of human reproductive technologies reflects a wider preoccupation with the repercussions of present technological development. The speed of technological development creates a gap between the production of new technologies and the possibility of their social assimilation, a gap that is not present in those societies based on custom and tradition where there is an equilibrium between technical activity and its cultural appropriation (Vanderburg 1987). The failure to integrate technology into its cultural context can lead to the understanding of technology as a 'magic force' responsible for the creation of marvellous mysterious mechanisms; a technology that is used more for its magical effect than its practical social value, transforming it from a 'means to an end' to an 'end in itself'. As the technological imperative states that 'everything that can be done must be done' (Ballard 1978), the self-justification of technological development can be particularly dangerous when humans are used as a means to obtain a technological end.

Medicine is a discipline where the danger of not considering the human perspective is especially worrying, particularly because of processes of scientific rationalization and technical practicality which dominate it. The traditional medical system presented an almost non-existent level of specialization, centred on the figure of the doctor.[4] This situation began to change with the consolidation of the hospital through its role during the industrial revolution. The concentration and examination of a considerable number of people made possible the identification of regularities in different types of sickness. During the eighteenth and nineteenth centuries the traditional theory of the equilibrium of solids and humours was progressively replaced by a modern conception of sickness where symptoms were compared across patients. In the nineteenth century, sickness gradually ceases to be patient-specific and the image of the body as a whole gives way to its conceptualization as a conglomeration of parts. This is reflected in the specialization of the medical institution according to specific parts of the body (such as cardiology), certain groups of patients (such as paediatrics) or certain treatment instruments (such as radiology).

Despite this transformation, medicine was still defined as an art at the beginning of the twentieth century, and physicians emphasized the harmony between individual, patient and environment (Rosenberg 1979). Medical practice was defined by three different principles (Sadler 1978): (a) practical indeterminability that required intuitive knowledge; (b) medical knowledge emerging from experience; and (c) the patient considered as a unique individual in need of a unique treatment. Medical knowledge was an art grounded in good education and sensitive practice. It has become progressively more scientific and technological.

Medicine deals with the production of medical knowledge, medical assistance and medical practitioners (Jamous and Peloille 1970). Justification for these productive processes is based on the premise of health production and illness eradication. Definitions of the body, its health and its forms of cure vary depending on the historical moment and as a function of the social context (Payer 1990). These definitions or forms of understanding constitute strong metaphors with a similar level of reality to the sickness itself (Sontag 1977, 1989). These understandings make sense inasmuch as they have a role in our everyday practices or, in other words, 'Illness – any illness – is meaningful as "illness" only to the extent that it has particular implications for us, as people, and not just as biological organisms' (Stainton-Rogers 1991: 31). These metaphors have been approached diachronically, looking at social history (Herzlich and Pierret 1984, 1986), or synchronically, exploring social understandings within a particular historical moment (Stainton-Rogers 1991).

Assisted reproductive technologies constitute a good example of the developments described above. They illustrate the process of specialization of the medical institution, in which the person as a whole is lost and intervention is directed towards the production of pregnancy by technical intervention on the body. There is also controversy on what kind of 'illness' is treated by these techniques. Their intervention seems directed more towards the fulfilment of a social demand, the establishment of a family, than to a 'cure' for an illness. Reproductive technologies can transform the structure of human nature and society and, therefore, they also open up the debate on the limits to scientific research and technical intervention. Although it can be argued that some kind of technological intervention in the reproductive field has always been present, the intensity of the transformation in recent years and, particularly, the possibilities emerging from the development of new reproductive practices suggest an important qualitative change. Nevertheless, what could be called the 'reproductive revolution' cannot be best characterized by its technological developments. Popularly known reproductive practices such as *in vitro* fertilization, surrogate motherhood or test tube babies do not represent a very important technological challenge, as they have been used for some time in animal farming. The revolutionary nature of these developments rests on the progressive extension of what is considered as a legitimate objective for medical intervention. The possibilities and dangers of these techniques have been discussed widely in the mass media and cause deep social concern.

It has been pointed out, for example, that assisted reproductive technologies add a new dimension to the development of the post-industrial society in a move from 'technologies of production' to 'technologies of reproduction' (McNeil 1990). This distinction highlights the role of certain technologies in the transformation of the division of work between men and women (Cockburn 1983); connections with population control (McLaren 1984); and the maintenance and reproduction of the power relationships between genders (Petchesky 1985). Another way of approaching the effects of these technologies is to look at the impact they have on women, considering both the possible effects on the body and the level of autonomy and decision-making they allow. The evaluation of reproductive technologies based on these two criteria can be used to differentiate between 'better' and 'worse' reproductive techniques (Stanworth 1987).

The social impact of the development of specific forms of reproductive technological intervention makes this topic especially relevant for a broader study of the relationship between science, technology and society (Pujol 1994). The specific issues explored are (a) limits of technological intervention; (b) ethical issues considered when humans are used as technological objects; and (c) the implications of technological innovation on our societal definitions (for example, what do we mean by 'mother' or 'progeny'?).

## Constructing discursive material

Discursive data, like any form of data, are not just 'obtained' by the researcher, but imply a process of construction through certain operations, such as transcribing, doing interviews or collecting documents. The researcher's perspective has an important influence on this process, in selecting certain material or generating certain themes in the interviews. Nevertheless, the procedure should ensure the presence of a certain degree of 'strangeness' in the material in order to make the relationship between researcher and data productive.

This study was based on group interviews, although varied cultural material was also collected as auxiliary material providing alternative readings (television programmes, newspapers and magazines). A group interview is a form of interaction close to everyday conversation, and it is a technique that minimizes the interviewer role. It facilitates the emergence of themes and topics not included in the interview agenda, increasing in this way the level of 'otherness' of the material. The make-up of the groups followed two criteria. First, the participants in the same group should have an expected shared understanding of the topic, and the participants were grouped in homogeneous categories (e.g. scientists, people who went through reproductive treatment). While heterogeneous groups lead to stereotyped answers, homogeneous groups expand and diversify a shared perspective. Second, participants met before the interview in order to facilitate verbal interaction and to become familiar with each other.

Allocation to groups was on the basis of participants' knowledge of and relationship with reproductive technologies (positive, negative or neutral). Forty-one participants from different parts of Catalonia (Spain) took part in nine discussion groups with a duration ranging from two to four hours.[5] The groups were labelled as (1) limited information; (2) some information without any contact; (3) successful reproductive treatment; (4, 5) unsuccessful reproductive treatment; (6) contact through friends or by being donors; (7) members of religious groups; (8) medical-scientific professionals; (9) active members of feminist groups.

A procedure derived from the automatic analysis of textual material (Lebart and Salem 1988; Íñiguez and Pujol 1993) was devised for the analysis, combining statistical information with the interpretation of transcripts of verbal interaction. This technique offers information on the structure of the textual data and provides characteristic fragments considering the words and word segments used (lexical forms). The steps in the analysis were as follows.

1 To divide the lexical forms into referential (reference to a subject), action and evaluative, and to calculate their frequencies.
2 To factor analyse the contingency table of persons against units of analysis (Lebart *et al.* 1977; Lebart and Salem 1988).

3 To select characteristic fragments for each participant based on the probability of appearance of a lexical form in a text or, alternatively, on the proximity of a lexical form to the corpus profile.

The first two steps, jointly with a reading of the whole material, provided a general overview of the interviews. The third step selected characteristic fragments based on their linguistic specificity. Because the researcher did not directly select the fragments, they provided a context where the interpretive perspective of the researcher could be challenged. The interpretation deals with pieces of verbal interaction selected through an independent criterion. The following section summarizes a set of readings emerging from the interpretation of the fragments (Pujol 1994).

## A reading

The interpretation suggested five strong themes underlying most of the textual material: (a) the dangers of technological development; (b) the social control of technology; (c) the need and desire to have a baby; (d) the repercussions of reproductive technologies on family relationships; (e) the experience of having a reproductive treatment.[6] Owing to space restrictions, each section starts with an English translation of a fragment exemplifying the material from which the reading emerged.[7]

### The dangers of technological development

#### Extract (PE19)

On one hand there is the need of the human being to know, to really show the knowledge, of what we really need, the knowledge of many things, and wanting to arrive at the centre, and we do not arrive. And I think we will not arrive. On the other, there are the interests; those people that really believe it; those scientists, that believe it, scientific development. I am in favour of scientific development; I do not believe we live better in nature, and living from daisies, and living . . . I do not agree with this. I support scientific development, but for what? The problem here, I think, are interests, strong economic interests, and of power. The issue of controlling science, of controlling power.[8]

The use of reproductive technologies implies the use of human beings as objects of technological intervention. The most prevalent form of justification of technology is articulated through the association between technology, progress and well-being: technology produces progress, the improvement of our social and natural environment, leading to improvements in our quality of life. The way in which 'improvement' is defined uses the person as the point of reference, using 'positive' when the consequences are beneficial for the person and 'negative' when they are not. Therefore, participants adopt an ethics of means–ends where the means are justified by the ends achieved, reproducing a dominant form of understanding technological development (Coolen 1987; Hottois 1987, 1990).

Those knowledges and technologies that are susceptible to being used on humans are potentially dangerous for the person, and the possibility of risk opens up a debate about the limits of this intervention. The participants locate the 'need for knowledge' as a natural human characteristic, while its technological application is located in the social realm. The social realm is perceived as 'corrupted' by economic and personal interests that can lead to a misuse of the 'natural need for knowledge'. Society has to be able to monitor and control the practical use of knowledge that can be transformed into a technical intervention on the person. This leads to a point of conflict as society corrupts knowledge but, at the same time, has to be able to control its own corruption.

Three main forms of arguing and justifying the dangers of technological intervention on human beings arise:

1 There is an analogy between the manipulation of and intervention on non-human organisms and intervention on humans, exploring the type of society that would result if those procedures were practised on humans. The central aspect in the comparison is the danger of the person being transformed into an instrumental object and susceptible to being used to satisfy social interests.

2 A second strategy creates an opposition between 'conscious effects' and 'unconscious effects' of technological intervention. Because any intervention has unexpected effects, unknown at the time of designing a particular technology, applied research has a certain degree of uncertainty. It is impossible to be absolutely certain prior to action of all possible material and social effects. This uncertainty increases in contexts where the intervention takes living creatures as objects owing to its structural and functional variability. Certain procedures valid for some individuals are not necessarily applicable to others.

3 Another theme is the opposition between the human ('little') and the technical ('big') dimensions. It reflects the loss of humanity through the use of technology, an aspect widely examined theoretically (see, for example, Ballard 1978; Vanderburg 1987). Technological development appears insensitive to a community's stock of traditional social rules.

## The social control of technology

### Extract (PER2)

I believe it is an aberration. It is basically an aberration. If an aberration exists, this is an example and a paradigm of what is an aberration.

One thing is what nature is doing for millions and millions of years, that people have to start creating something that nature keeps doing every second, it seems so absurd to me. It is an aberration. It can only have aberrant consequences. And there are, there are. In the press, I tell you, there were simians that they are not simians or humans . . . , as in a particular moment then . . . This was in the press. And not in the tabloids but in the quality papers . . . What happens is that because motives, as there are many created interests there, then having a half-human . . . this would be the word because I think that this the problem here is that it is a half-human. Then, having half-humans to clean the house, half-humans as miners, half-humans doing certain things . . .[9]

Criticisms of reproductive technologies use the economic aspects of its practice as a central argument. There is a strong resistance to accepting the instrumental use of human life in terms of efficacy and efficiency; a use that could lead to the creation of forms of semi-human life to increase the productivity of certain economic areas. This theme is structured in terms of natural–social, where reproduction is located in the natural-neutral realm while its commercial use is located in the social-moral one. The dichotomy between natural and social acquires special importance when one is dealing with surrogate motherhood, where the social field is seen as responsible for the rupture of natural maternity.

The separation between natural and social is at the root of the problem with instrumental usage, as the natural-neutral values are translated into the personal and economic interests of the social. It is in this context that reproductive technologies are perceived in more negative terms and are labelled as 'inhuman' or 'aberration'. The possibility of an instrumental use of the human being raises questions about the mechanisms of control that should be applied to it. Participants frequently adopt an optimistic perspective, seeing the person as capable of being responsible for the technical developments produced. This position argues that there will always be a new technological development that solves old technical problems.

### The need and the desire to have a child

#### Extract (PE38)

No, you cannot deny it. And I also think that you cannot forget the psychological dimension. It is not something that is socially influenced. Things do not fall from the social to the biological in this way, but there is the entire the psychological framework, the adaptation of the social to the person, and it is a complicated framework. Then, the desire of the woman is fundamental. One cannot forget that that woman wants to have a baby.[10]

### Extract (PER8)

And especially what I have said at the beginning. A couple without a child is not a couple. Do you know what I mean? There are couples that go all right, but when one can truly see the personality of each one, of each couple, is when there is a child. To see responsibilities or what have you said of 'father' and 'son' or 'mother' and 'daughter', if the mother takes all the responsibilities or the father is also there. I believe it is there that one starts to really know the couple. Not before because until then everything is 'very nice'. There is no responsibility. Well, there is responsibility but the major responsibility is a child. And it is strong for couples, that you believe you are prepared to educate the child, everyday you learn something else . . . .[11]

Users of reproductive technologies, despite a positive or negative account, explicitly deny (although some social pressures are suggested) that the desire to have a child has a social dimension. Emphasizing the natural character of the desire justifies the need to use reproductive technologies as a way of artificially accomplishing a natural function biologically inscribed, a justification disabled when the desire is located in the social realm. Different authors have explained the concealing of the pressures to have a child through the internalization of the social conventions and definitions about women's biological functions (Crowe 1987; Pujal 1991).

Even though having a baby is construed as natural, a dimension of responsibility is added for the user of reproductive technologies compared with a 'normal' parent. The need is located in the realm of nature, but its fulfilment is in the social realm, meaning that it is necessary to introduce higher standards compared to 'having a child naturally'. In this context, a dichotomy between knowledge and desire begins to emerge. Knowledge allows modulation of the desire, and the greater the knowledge, the greater the awareness of the limits of this desire. The dichotomy 'to know' versus 'to wish' also emerges when adoption is brought into the discussion, and it locates the ultimate moral responsibility for the decision to have a child within the person herself. Only women can know if the desire responds to a manifestation of her nature or the personal satisfaction of a fanciful wish.

The social dimension of the need to have a baby comes from the definition of what constitutes a relationship. Children affirm the relationship, transforming a 'couple' into a 'family'; they constitute a visible sign of the relationship and personify the commitment to perpetuate the alliance. To have a child is to make the relationship more real, it constitutes a necessary step, like living together, to affirm the union.

## The family

### Extract (PER2)

Then, in a case like this, what is at stake is the ownership of the child. Then the child is a victim of both the father and the mother. Most of the time it is a victim of the father and the mother because what parents want is to have ownership of the child. And obviously, it does not matter where the child ends up, it will become an object of exchange ... If a rich family has a certain amount of property, what it cannot do is to leave it to a charity. It has to leave it to their children. And those children cannot be of another race ... They have to be their own children; or at least half their children, like in the case of surrogate mothers, at least half of it. I think it is crazy, a delirium.[12]

The impact of reproductive technologies on the institution of the family is an important and persistent theme. The consequences of allowing the possibility of unconventional family structures, such as gay couples with children, develops into a criticism against reproductive technologies. Despite the criticism, participants highlight how these techniques reproduce the traditional model of the family in terms of 'couple with two children', a model that could be transformed in the near future into 'couple with a boy and a girl' because of these technologies. The reproduction of normative forms of family structure by reproductive technologies is a criticism developed in the literature (see, for example, Stranthern 1992).

Participants perceive that reproductive technologies mimic the traditional family structure in terms of relationships of property both personal ('to have my own child') and economical ('inheritance'). These technologies guarantee a certain degree of physical resemblance between parents and progeny, reproducing family models better than other procedures, such as adoption. Adoption is used as an example of the issues arising when the family structure is not reproduced: (a) problems of inheritance; (b) physical or psychological problems from the biological parents; (c) the need of special preparation for a family to adopt a child. Despite these arguments, reproductive technologies appear as an artificial procedure, and this is particularly visible in those participants who have gone through reproductive treatment. This is reflected in the transcripts in different ways: first, the reiterative affirmation that the child obtained through these techniques is as 'normal' as others; second, the perception of relational problems with other members of the family because of the negativity associated with the 'artificial baby'; third, the need for a good couple relationship that would not be affected by the 'noise' generated by the treatment.

## The experience

### Extract (PE15)

In a similar way to motivate other people that have problems to say 'no, it is not that bad . . .' Yes, from my perspective I think so. To tell our experience, that we have had our issues, but I mean, the positive result has been that it has been worth going through all this period to achieve a target. What is going on is that the technique does not guarantee that everybody will achieve a baby, but there is a percentage, some techniques, that depending on the causes, but to the majority of the people I would suggest going through it. Yes.[13]

### Extract (PE17)

Let's say a forgotten experience. This has been a lapse, a period in our lives around which we have set brackets because it has been quite painful . . . It has been . . . yes, painful. You were not living your life. You were forced into certain behaviours, into certain sets of actions, certain drugs. To prescriptions by the doctors that you feel all right with them or you did not. Normally you did not . . . It is something more complex than when the doctor says 'at thirty-five minutes past seven and you have to do this or that', or you do not do it . . .[14]

Three different accounts have emerged in relation to the experience with reproductive technologies. The first one has its origin in the direct contact with the treatment and uses direct experiential knowledge as justification of moral decisions. Participants have to justify the involvement with the treatment, a warrant that becomes particularly important as it constitutes a rupture with the tradition in which the person is living. The ethical value of the decision comes from a position of involvement with the treatment, using experience as a non-rational form of ethically justifying actions. In some cases there appears an instrumental form of warrant in terms of the personal consequences of the treatment, never as a generalizing principle but in individual and personal terms, such as 'it worked for me'. In this kind of position the negative aspects derived from the experience with the treatment emerge. It highlights the painful adaptation of everyday life to the demands and rigidity of the treatment. It also draws attention to the temporal and economic costs of the treatment. It has to be mentioned that no reference is made to the dangers of the treatment for the woman's health, dangers often highlighted in the literature (see, for example, Cabau 1986; Laborie 1987; Crowe 1990).

A second similar account arises, also coming from personal experience. While the previous one deals with the direct experience, this is about the experience of the distance between the end of the treatment and the present moment. It highlights the difference between what they thought during the treatment and what they think now, and it is particularly important when the treatment was not successful.

A final kind of experience comes through the appropriation of others' experiences. This account, from an external position, points to the extraordinary effort of women to overcome their biological limits. This perspective criticizes the construction of the desire to have a child in terms of a biological necessity and highlights the negative effects that have been reported (e.g. Crowe 1987), such as the dynamics of expectation frustration to which women under treatment are subjected. This narrative is especially important, as it is connected with a broader account in terms of success or failure of women performing their defined role in society; that is to say, a success or failure of her biology.

## Conclusions

This chapter has considered interpretation as a productive relationship between researcher and text, motivated by a need to intervene in the world. The relationship between the reader's suspicion towards technological development and the extracts narrating views and experiences of technological development and reproductive technologies has produced a reading with different implications. One of the basic strategies in the justification of technological development constitutes the association between progress and human well-being, a strategy based on an anthropomorphic ethics of means–ends. The technological use of human beings introduces disturbance into the equation when human well-being can be jeopardized as a result of our pursuit of this aim. This process is also affected by the perception of a human need for knowledge as 'natural', leaving the possibility of a 'zero option', of refusing new research, as a form of utopia. This type of argumentation can be found in some of the environmental pressure groups, where the warrants for taking care of the environment are based on the advantages it has to humans, and where research is pursued as a form of knowing the right type of action. In place of this conceptualization, where beings are relevant as far as they are of use to humans, new forms of ethics need to be developed where consideration is not given to the 'benefits' of certain forms of technological action. The distinction between the 'human' and the 'technological' is also at the root of the contradictions emerging when one is talking about the social control of technological development.

When technology is considered as 'non-social', the subject–object dichotomy appears and it is possible that technology can be 'socially monitored'. It is the introduction of the social character of technological action that endangers the stability of this dichotomy, and this is the point where new forms of understanding need to be developed. An 'alternative modernity' can be built based on the introduction of cultural forms of understanding in the evaluation of technological development (Feenberg 1995), the rejection of science neutrality and the redefinition of instrumental elements (like non-humans) as active actors in technological productions (Latour 1991).

Surrogate motherhood is a reproductive procedure where the above dichotomies are more clearly displayed. Being one of the technically simpler procedures, it has nevertheless received the strongest criticisms. This is even more remarkable if we take into consideration that bearing a baby for other people is not a new phenomenon (Zipper and Sevenhuijsen 1987). To understand the criticisms of this technique, two aspects have to be taken into consideration. First, the introduction of technological procedures transfers the practice from the private to the public realm by introducing the medical institution as a necessary mediator in the reproductive process. Private agreements give way to a formal contract under public scrutiny through the judicial and administrative systems. Second, surrogate motherhood introduces society into an area traditionally defined as 'natural': the relationship of the mother and the child during pregnancy. The justifications for using reproductive technologies reflect the oppositions underlying the criticisms of surrogate motherhood. The turn to reproductive technologies is justified by the natural need to have a baby. However, because technology is a human activity, its participation in the reproductive process introduces the social realm. Technology creates an opportunity to redefine the meaning of having a baby. Instead of being the expression of a 'natural need', having a baby can conceal a purely egoistic wish. This form of understanding is particularly important given the 'naturalness' implied when these technologies are not involved. It could be important at this point to emphasize the cultural relativity in the understanding of reproduction and the different functions reproductive technologies have (Stranthern 1992). It may be the case that these technological developments mask the perpetuation of our culturally anchored model of 'traditional family' under the guise of solving a personal need. Institutional policies often reproduce societal prejudices, and a public discussion about the value of the alternatives to these technologies, such as adoption, should be encouraged.

This latter point is particularly relevant when we take into account the personal and economic costs of reproductive treatments, particularly when they are unsuccessful. The use of reproductive technologies should solve social problems instead of being a default option which is easily available. One of their perverse effects is to force women to make reproductive decisions (Katz Rothman 1984). Women have to choose between different reproductive options, excluding the option of not choosing. Society develops in such a way that reproduction has to be controlled and monitored (Rowland 1987). Reproductive decisions have a direct effect on women in areas such as educational and work opportunities, personal relationships,

Table 5.1 Aspects of the dichotomy between 'natural' and 'social'

| Natural (neutral) | Social (moral) |
| --- | --- |
| The need for knowledge represented by the scientist | The social corruption of knowledge by technology |
| The experience of assisted reproductive treatment | The view of the treatment |
| Natural reproduction, sterility | Assisted reproductive technologies |
| The desire to have a child | The responsibility of having a child |
| Traditional family | New forms of families |
| Love and responsibility of the progenitors | Economic and power interests of the progenitors |
| Human-being-in-itself | Human being as a means to a technological end |

level of income, emotional and affective stability, and they affect their general social and economic situation. Reproductive technologies appear as an opportunity for women to adapt to society instead of society adapting to women's needs. It is paradoxical that the technological option is justified in terms of fulfilling a 'natural' need. Through this reading, the important role of the dichotomy 'natural' versus 'social' in the discourse on reproductive technologies is becoming increasingly apparent. The different aspects of this opposition can be characterized and summarized in Table 5.1.

The dichotomy between the natural and the social through which the discourses on reproductive technologies are structured is also one of the unfinished debates in the social sciences about the predominance of nature or culture. Having a child can be interpreted as something inscribed within human nature or as the expression of a certain social structure. Reproductive technologies are associated either with socio-economic interests or with the solution to the natural need to have a child. The opposition between 'nature' and 'culture' can be seen as a heritage of the Cartesian and Kantian paradigms. Under these perspectives, nature, the Kantian thing-in-itself, is characterized as independent and external to the human mind. Human beings produce knowledge about nature, a knowledge that will transform external nature and will sustain the social. The dichotomy of natural versus social constitutes a key element in the understanding of the controversial character of reproductive technologies and reveals the limits of such division. Reproductive technologies challenge the division as nature loses its externality and independence. The person is both the object and subject of technology, product and producer, unnatural and asocial. The problematization of the natural versus social debate points to the need to generate ways of understanding reproductive technologies which surpass duality and to the importance of shifting from dual approaches, such as the Cartesian or Kantian, towards unitary paradigms such as the Hegelian or Heideggerian.[15]

## Acknowledgements

This work has been possible thanks to the scholarship Batista I Roca (Comissionat per a Universitats i Recerca de la Generalitat de Catalunya). I would also like to thank Carla Willig, Angel Gordo and Marisela Montenegro for their helpful comments and suggestions.

## Notes

1 Another much less popular quote would soften its force: 'What cannot be said exists. It displays itself, it is what is mystical' (Wittgenstein 1921: §6.522).
2 Intentionality has been taken as an example because it is a central concept in speech-act theory (Austin 1962; Searle 1969). This theory develops fundamental aspects of Wittgenstein's work and has influenced important theoretical and methodological developments such as the theory of communicative action (Habermas 1981) or discourse analysis (Potter and Wetherell 1987).
3 The *International Journal of Transdisciplinary Studies* constitutes an example of the effort to move outside disciplinary boundaries.
4 In England, for example, the *Royal College of Physicians* was in charge of controlling the medical profession and providing legal licences for practitioners (Clark 1964). To obtain the licence the candidates passed an oral exam focused on physiological instead of medical knowledge. Medical practitioners at the end of the eighteenth century were mostly known for their intelligence and elegance rather than for their medical knowledge (Carr-Saunders and Wilson 1933; Reader 1966).
5 I would like to thank Ana Garai for the help offered with the interviews.
6 For a full description of themes and list of fragments see Pujol (1994).
7 The fragments do not identify the 'type' of person (e.g. scientist or religious person), since the focus of the analysis is not the person but on the discourse produced.
8 por una parte está la necesidad entre comillas del ser humano de conocer, de realmente mostrar el conocimiento, o sea lo que realmente nos falta, el conocimiento de mogollón de historias, y el querer llegar al núcleo; y que no se llega. Y es que yo pienso que no se va a llegar. Por otro lado están los intereses; por un lado está la gente que realmente se lo cree, esos científicos, tal que se lo creen, el desarrollo científico, yo estoy por el desarrollo científico, cuidado, yo no creo que vivamos mejor en la naturaleza, y viviendo de las margaritas, y viviendo . . . Yo no estoy de acuerdo con eso, yo apoyo el desarrollo científico, pero, ¿para qué?, El problema de ahí, yo creo que son los intereses, intereses económicos muy fuertes y de poder, el rollo del control de la ciencia, es el rollo del control del poder . . .

9 Yo creo que es una aberración. Básicamente una aberración. Si existe una aberración, eso quizás sería un ejemplo y un paradigma de lo que es una aberración. O sea, una cosa que la naturaleza lleva haciendo desde hace millones y millones de años, que el hombre tenga que empezar a crear una cosa que la naturaleza cada segundo está realizando, me parece que es tan absurdo; es aberración. Solamente puede tener consecuencias de aberración. Y ya las hay, ya las hay. En la prensa, ya te digo, que salían unos monos que no son ni monos ni hombres, que son como mongoles, que ya en un momento dado pues . . . No, si esto salió en la prensa. Y no la prensa sensacionalista, sino que salió en la prensa . . . Lo que pasa es que por motivos de que hay muchos intereses creados ahí, pues tener un semi-humano – sería la palabra porque creo que el problema de esto es que es semi-humano. Entonces meter semi-humanos a limpiar la casa, semi-humanos a bajar a las minas, semi-humanos a hacer ciertas cosas . . .

10 No, no puedes decir no, y además yo creo que no se puede olvidar la dimensión psicológica, no es un cosa que está socialmente influida; las cosas no caen de lo social a lo biológico así, sino que está todo el entramado psicológico que es la adaptación de lo social a la propia persona, y es un entramado complicadísimo, entonces el deseo de la mujer es fundamental, no te puedes olvidar que esa mujer quiere tener un hijo . . .

11 . . . Y sobretodo lo que he dicho al principio. Una pareja sin crío no es pareja; para mí. ¿a ver si me entendéis? Cuidado, hay parejas que muy bien y tal, pero cuando se ve verdaderamente el la personalidad de cada uno, de cada pareja, es cuando hay un hijo. A ver las responsabilidades, o lo que has dicho tú de 'padre' y 'hijo' o 'madre y hija' si la que se lleva todo el trabajo es la madre o si el padre también está ahí. Ahí creo que se empieza a conocer verdaderamente la pareja. Hasta entonces no, porque hasta entonces todo es muy bonito. No hay ninguna responsabilidad. Hay responsabilidad y tal, pero que la mayor responsabilidad es un crío. Y es fuerte que parejas, que te creas válido para educarlo y tal, es que cada día aprendes una historieta que dices, 'vaya tela ¿no?' De dónde me sale a mí ahora el microbio éste. No sé.

12 entonces, en un caso así lo que se trata es quién tiene la propiedad del niño. Entonces el niño es un víctima, tanto del padre como de la madre. La mayoría de las veces es una víctima del padre y de la madre porque los padres lo que quieren es tener, tener la propiedad del niño. Y él, pues evidentemente, caiga en unas manos o caiga en otras manos, evidentemente, va a ser un objeto de intercambio . . . Si una familia normalmente rica tiene una acumulación lo que no puede hacer es dejárselo a una fundación. Se lo tiene que dejar a sus hijos. Y si estos hijos no pueden ser un negrito, ni puede ser . . . Tienen que ser sus hijos. O por lo menos, la mitad de sus hijos – el tema de las madres de alquiler – al menos la mitad. Yo pienso que es un delirio. Un delirio.

13 de una forma motivar a otra gente que tenga problemas de decir "no, no es tanto . . ." Sí. Por mi parte pienso que sí. De explicarles nuestra experiencia vivida, que hemos tenido las nuestras pequeñas cosas pero quiero decir, que el resultado positivo ha sido que ha valido la pena pasar toda esta época para conseguir un objetivo. Lo que pasa es que esta técnica no te asegura que todos conseguirán un crío, pero que hay un porcentaje, unas técnicas, que dependerá de las causas pero a la mayoría de gente les aconsejaría que lo pasaran. Sí.

14 Buf!... Digamos más bien experiencia olvidada. Esto ha sido un lapso, un período en nuestra vida que hemos puesto un paréntesis porque ha sido bastante penoso... Ha sido más bien, sí, penoso también. No estabas viviendo tu vida. Estabas obligado a ciertos comportamientos, a cierta serie de acciones, a ciertos medicamentos, a prescripciones por parte de los médicos que te iban o no te iban. Normalmente no te iban. Con un... Es una cosa más complicada que cuando el médico dice "a las siete y treinta y cinco has de hacer esto o lo otro", o lo dejas de hacer.

15 The work of Donna Haraway constitutes an example of this approach (Haraway 1991). She suggests the cyborg as metaphor and combines within the same identity some of the oppositions structuring Western metaphysics.

## References

Austin, J. L. (1962) *How to Do Things with Words.* Cambridge, MA: Harvard University Press.

Ballard, E. G. (1978) *Man and Technology: Toward the Measurement of a Culture.* Duquesne: Duquesne University Press.

Bhaskar, R. (1975) *A Realist Theory of Science.* Brighton: Harvester Press.

Bhaskar, R. (1989) *Reclaiming Reality: A Critical Introduction to Contemporary Philosophy.* London: Verso.

Billig, M. (1987) *Arguing and Thinking: A Rhetorical Approach to Social Psychology.* Cambridge: Cambridge University Press.

Bleicher, J. (1980) *Contemporary Hermeneutics: Hermeneutics as Method, Philosophy and Critique.* London: Routledge & Kegan Paul.

Brown, S. R. (1980) *Political Subjectivity: Applications of Q-methodology in Political Science.* New Haven, CT: Yale University Press.

Cabau, A. (1986) Dangers des inducteurs de l'ovulation, *La Lettre du Gynecologues,* 45: 38–64.

Carr-Saunders, A. M. and Wilson, P. A. (1933) *The Professions.* Oxford: Clarendon Press.

Clark, G. N. (1964) *A History of the Royal College of Physicians.* Harmondsworth: Penguin.

Cockburn, C. (1983) *Brothers: Male Dominance and Technological Change.* London: Pluto Press.

Coolen, T. M. T. (1987) Philosophical anthropology and the problem of responsibility in technology. In P. T. Durbin (ed.) *Technology and Responsibility.* Dordrecht: Reidel.

Crowe, C. (1987) Women want it: in vitro fertilisation and women's motivations for participation. In P. Spallone and D. L. Steinberg (eds) *Made to Order: The Myth of Reproductive and Genetic Progress.* Oxford: Pergamon Press.

Crowe, C. (1990) Whose mind over whose matter? Women, in vitro fertilisation and the development of scientific knowledge. In M. McNeil, I. Varcoe and S. Yearley (eds) *The New Reproductive Technologies.* London: Macmillan.

Curt, B. C. (1994) *Textuality and Tectonics: Troubling Social and Psychological Science.* Buckingham: Open University Press.

Derrida, J. (1973) *Speech and Phenomena, and Other Essays on Husserl's Theory of Signs*. Evanston, IL: Northwestern University Press.

Derrida, J. (1977) *Signature Event Context, Glyph*, vol. 1. Baltimore: Johns Hopkins University Press.

Feenberg, A. (1995) *Alternative Modernity: The Technical Turn in Philosophy and Social Theory*. Berkeley: University of California Press.

Gadamer, H. (1960) *Truth and Method*. New York: Continuum.

Habermas, J. (1981) *The Theory of Communicative Action, Volume 1: Reason and the Rationalization of Society*. London: Heinemann.

Haraway, D. J. (1991) *Simians, Cyborgs and Women: The Reinvention of Nature*. London: Free Association Books.

Harris, W. V. (1988) *Interpretative Acts: In Search of Meaning*. Oxford: Clarendon Press.

Herzlich, C. and Pierret, J. (1984) *Illness and Self in Society*. London: Johns Hopkins University Press.

Herzlich, C. and Pierret, J. (1985) The social construction of the patient: patients and illnesses in other ages, *Social Science and Medicine*, 20(2): 145–51.

Herzlich, C. and Pierret, J. (1986) Illness: from causes to meaning. In C. Currer and M. Stacey (eds) *Concepts of Health, Illness and Disease: A Comparative Perspective*. Leamington Spa: Berg.

Herzlich, C. and Pierret, J. (1989) The construction of a social phenomenon: AIDS in the French press, *Social Science and Medicine*, 29(11): 1235–42.

Hottois, G. (1987) Technoscience: nihilistic power versus a new ethical consciousness. In P. T. Durbin (ed.) *Technology and Responsibility*. Dordrecht: Reidel.

Hottois, G. (1990) *El Paradigma Bioético: Una ética para la tecnociencia*. Barcelona: Anthropos.

Íñiguez, L. and Pujol, J. (1993) Preliminary statistical analysis of textual data: an example with the discourse of new reproductive technologies. In EAESP *Social Psychology in Europe*. Lisbon: Ediçoes Cosmos.

Jamous, H. and Peloille, B. (1970) Professions as self-perpetuating systems: changes in the French university-hospital system. In J. A. Jackson (ed.) *Professions and Professionalization*. Cambridge: Cambridge University Press.

Jones, H. W., Acosta, A. A., Andrews, M. C., Garcia, J. E., Jones, G. S., Mantzavinos, T., McDowell, J., Sandow, B. A., Veeck, L. and Whibley, T. W. (1983) What is a pregnancy? A question for programs of in vitro fertilization, *Fertility and Sterility*, 40(6): 728–33.

Katz Rothman, B. (1984) The meanings of choice in reproductive technology. In R. Arditti, R. Duelly Klein and S. Minden (eds) *Test-tube Women. What Future for Motherhood?* London: Pandora Press.

Kearney, R. (1984) *Dialogues with Contemporary Continental Thinkers*. Manchester: Manchester University Press.

Kvale, S. (1983) The qualitative research interview: a phenomenological and hermeneutical mode of understanding, *Journal of Phenomenological Psychology*, 14(2): 171–96.

Laborie, F. (1987) Looking for mothers you only find foetuses. In P. Spallone and D. L. Steinberg (eds) *Made to Order: The Myth of Reproductive and Genetic Progress*. Oxford: Pergamon Press.

Latour, B. (1991) *We Have Never Been Modern*. London: Harvester Wheatsheaf.

Lebart, L. and Morineau, A. (1984) *SPAD. Système Portable Pour l'Analyse des Données Statistiques*. Paris: Dunod.

Lebart, L., Morineau, A. and Warwick, K. M. (1977) *Multivariate Descriptive Analysis, Correspondence Analysis and Related Techniques for Large Matrices*. New York: John Wiley & Sons.

Lebart, L. and Salem, A. (1988) *Analyse Statistique des Données Textuelles*. Paris: Dunod.

McLaren, A. (1984) *Reproductive Rituals: The Perception of Fertility and Birth from the Sixteenth Century to the Nineteenth*. London: Methuen.

McNeil, M. (1990) Reproductive technologies: a new terrain for the sociology of technology. In M. McNeil, I. Varcoe and S. Yearley (eds) *The New Reproductive Technologies*. London: Macmillan.

Parker, I. (1992) *Discourse Dynamics: Critical Analysis for Social and Individual Psychology*. London: Routledge.

Payer, L. (1990) *Medicine and Culture*. London: Victor Gollancz.

Petchesky, R. P. (1985) *Abortion and Woman's Choice: The State, Sexuality and Reproductive Freedom*. London: Verso.

Potter, J. and Wetherell, M. (1987) *Discourse and Social Psychology*. London: Sage.

Pujal, M. (1990) Influencia minoritaria y nuevas tecnologías, in J. M. Peiró (comp.) *Trabajo, organizaciones y márqueting social, Volume 5*. Barcelona: PPU.

Pujal, M. (1991) Poder, saber, naturaleza: la triangulación 'masculina' de la mujer y su deconstrucción, unpublished Mphil thesis, Univesitat Autònoma de Barcelona.

Pujol, J. (1994) *Retórica científica y técnicas de reproducción asistida*. Bellaterra: Publicacions de la UAB (microfiche).

Pye-Smith, P. H. (1900) Medicine as a science and medicine as an art, *Lancet*, 2: 302–5.

Reader, W. J. (1966) *The Rise of the Professional Classes in 19th Century England*. London: Weidenfeld & Nicholson.

Ricoeur, P. (1981) *Hermeneutics and the Human Sciences*. Cambridge: Cambridge University Press.

Rorty, R. (1967) Introduction: metaphilosophical difficulties of linguistic philosophy. In R. Rorty (ed.) *The Linguistic Turn*. Chicago: The University of Chicago Press.

Rosenberg, C. (1979) The therapeutic revolution: medicine, meaning and social change in nineteenth-century America. In M. J. Vogel and C. E. Rosenberg (eds) *The Therapeutic Revolution: Essays in the Social History of American Medicine*. Philadelphia: University of Pennsylvania Press.

Rowland, R. (1987) Of women born, but for how long? The relationship of women to the new reproductive technologies and the issue of choice. In P. Spallone and D. L. Steinberg (eds) *Made to Order: The Myth of Reproductive and Genetic Progress*. Oxford: Pergamon Press.

Sadler, J. (1978) Ideologies of 'art' and 'science' in medicine: the transition from medical care to the application of technique in the British medical profession. In W. Krohn, E. T. Layton and P. Weingart (eds) *The Dynamics of Science and Technology*. Dordrecht: Reidel.

Searle, J. (1969) *Speech Acts*. Cambridge: Cambridge University Press.

Sontag, S. (1977) *Illness as Methaphor*. New York: Farrar, Straus & Giroux.

Sontag, S. (1989) *AIDS and Its Metaphors*. London: Penguin.

Stainton-Rogers, R. (1995) Q-methodology. In J. Smith, R. Harré and L. V. Langenhove (eds) *Rethinking Methods in Psychology*. London: Sage.

Stainton-Rogers, W. (1991) *Explaining Health and Illness*. London: Harvester Wheatsheaf.

Stanworth, M. (1987) Reproductive technologies and the deconstruction of motherhood. In M. Stanworth (ed.) *Reproductive Technologies: Gender, Motherhood and Medicine*. Cambridge: Polity Press.

Stranthern, M. (1992) *Reproducing the Future: Anthropology, Kinship and the New Reproductive Technologies*. Manchester: Manchester University Press.

Thompson, J. B. (1981) *Critical Hermeneutics: A Study in the Thought of Paul Ricoeur and Jürgen Habermas*. Cambridge: Cambridge University Press.

Vanderburg, W. H. (1987) Technique and responsibility: think globally, act locally, according to Jacques Ellul. In P. T. Durbin (ed.) *Technology and Responsibility*. Dordrecht: Reidel.

Wittgenstein, L. (1921) *Traetatus Logico-philosophicus*. (London: Routledge and Kegan Paul, paperback edn 1974).

Zipper, J. and Sevenhuijsen, S. (1987) Surrogacy: feminist notions of motherhood reconsidered. In M. Stanworth (ed.) *Reproductive Technologies: Gender, Motherhood and Medicine*. Cambridge: Polity Press.

# 6 Discourse analysis and sex education

## CARLA WILLIG

At Hackney Free and Parochial School they know that sex education is necessary. Teachers once asked some 16-year-olds what they knew about sex. Half of them believed that you could not get pregnant the first time. One thought that foreplay was four people having sex together. Another said that casual sex was watching television and deciding to have sex.

(Beckett 1993)

Sex education is generally understood to refer to the process by which ignorance in relation to sexual matters is dispelled. The need for sex education is frequently demonstrated by drawing attention to the pervasiveness of myths and misinformation about sex, and by reference to high levels of teenage pregnancies. More recently, the reduction of sexually transmitted diseases (STDs) in general and HIV transmission in particular has become another key objective of sex education. This has meant that sex education is now targeted at adults as well as its more traditional audience of older children and teenagers.[1]

There has been much controversy surrounding sex education in the UK in recent years. The last Conservative government (1979–97) introduced a number of measures which restricted the nature and content of sex education in Britain. These included Section 28 of the Local Government Act, which proscribed the 'promotion of homosexuality', and introduced a new legal requirement to teach sex education within a clear moral framework and the right for parents to withdraw their children from sex education lessons. Such restrictions were informed by moral-political as well as economic agendas (Durham 1997). The government sought to reduce welfare spending and to shift social responsibilities from the state to the nuclear family. The debates provoked by the government's interventions in sex education revolved around the relationship between knowledge about sex and sexual practice. While supporters of the government's approach argued that too much knowledge was likely to encourage young people to have sex, opponents countered that ignorance encouraged sexual experimentation and risk-taking (e.g. Beckett 1993; MacLeod 1995). Interestingly, both sides tended to share the view that sex education should aim to delay the onset of young people's sexual careers. However, the liberal position also acknowledged that this may not be achievable, and that sexual safety must therefore remain a priority.

## Psychology and sex education

Social psychologists have studied the relationship between knowledge, attitudes and behaviour for many years. Ever since LaPiere's (1934) classic study revealing a mismatch between attitudes and behaviour, psychologists have been aware that the relationship between cognitions and actions is not a straightforward one and that behaviour cannot be predicted on the basis of attitudes alone (e.g. Wicker 1969). For example, there is a wealth of research which has demonstrated that accurate knowledge about the risks of HIV infection does not necessarily lead to the adoption of safer sex practices (e.g. SSRU 1994; Ogden 1996; Pitts 1996; Wellings and Field 1996). A recent review of published evaluations of the effectiveness of AIDS education programmes came to the conclusion that sound and effective interventions tended to be skill-based, and delivered by peers or clinical psychologists within community settings (SSRU 1994). However, most AIDS education programmes adopt a simple information delivery mode, where lectures, videos and question-and-answer sessions provide the facts about HIV transmission and prevention. Psychological research findings have not informed much AIDS education practice.

## Social cognition and behaviour change

It would be wrong to suggest that psychological research has not had any impact upon health promotion practice. Social cognition theory, in particular, has been used in order to design interventions aimed at bringing about behavioural change (e.g. Conner et al. 1994). Social cognition theory proposes that people's actions are informed by their perceptions of social reality and that behavioural intentions will change as a result of changes in social cognitions. Social cognitions include beliefs, attitudes and expectations about self (e.g. self-efficacy) and others (e.g. normative beliefs). Health promotion interventions informed by a social cognition framework aim to change cognitions through the provision of information. For example, beliefs about susceptibility to HIV infection are challenged through epidemiological information, normative beliefs are modified through socially desirable role models, self-efficacy is increased through examples of ordinary people's successful behaviour change. More recently, social cognition theorists (e.g. Abraham and Sheeran 1994) have included participatory interventions (e.g. role play) in order to change cognitions such as perceived self-efficacy.

Social cognition models have received limited empirical support. They can account for up to 50 per cent of the variance in declared intentions to adopt health behaviours but only control up to 20 per cent of the variance in actual behaviour (e.g. Conner and Norman 1995; Marks *et al.* (in press)). Social cognition models have been criticized for their preoccupation with behavioural intentions and their lack of concern with actual behaviour (e.g. Abraham and Sheeran 1993), their neglect of the role of social context in health behaviour (e.g. Conner 1993), the rigidity of research designs used to test them (e.g. Ingham 1993), their conceptualization of the individual as rational decision-maker (e.g. Ingham *et al.* 1991, 1992) and their lack of concern with the direct effects of material and physical factors upon health behaviours (e.g. Marks *et al.* (in press)).

## Psychology and sexual practice

The application of psychological research to the practice of sex education has been both limited and limiting. Highly relevant research findings about the complex relationship between knowledge, attitudes and behaviour tend to be by-passed in the design of sex education programmes, while an individualistic and rationalistic social cognition approach continues to dominate psychological research into sexual behaviour.

Social constructionist approaches to the study of sexual discourse and practice are concerned with meanings. It is argued that in order to understand people's actions, we need to know what they mean. Sexual practices carry symbolic meanings and they constitute a form of communication. For example, unprotected sex can signal high levels of commitment to a relationship (Hollway 1989), whereas condom use can communicate a lack of trust in one's partner (Willig 1997). From a social constructionist perspective, therefore, sexual acts are not the consequence of a cost–benefit analysis based upon an individual's social cognitions, but rather a way of positioning oneself within a network of social meanings and significations.

Such a conceptualization has implications for sex education. First, it suggests that an individual's cognitions about sex cannot be changed in isolation. Changes in individual sexual behaviour require shifts in discourses surrounding sex and sexuality. Second, appeals to 'rationality' are not helpful, since different actions are 'rational' from within different frameworks of meaning. For example, if my aim is to prove that I am committed to a particular relationship, then unsafe sex may indeed be the rational choice. Third, the primary aims of sex education (i.e. to promote and encourage safe and responsible sexual relations) may not be compatible with dominant constructions of sexuality and sexual relationships. In order to be effective, sex education may have to challenge institutionalized discourses and practices, and thus become an explicitly political project.

This chapter presents a discourse analysis of heterosexual adults' talk about sexual activity and sexual safety within the context of HIV/AIDS. Discursive constructions of sexual activity and sexual relationships are identified and their implications for safer sex education are explored. The chapter concludes by formulating recommendations for discourse-based sex education.

## Discourse analysis of talk about sex and safety

In a series of recent papers, I have explored discursive constructions of sexual safety and risk-taking (Willig 1995, 1997, 1998). Analyses presented in these papers were based upon semi-structured interviews with 16 heterosexual men and women, aged 22–56 years. Participants were interviewed individually, and each interview lasted approximately one hour. The interview agenda included questions about the nature of HIV and AIDS, and its social, political and personal implications, including sexual risk-taking and sexual relationships. All interviews were tape-recorded and transcribed. In this chapter, I aim to integrate the results from these earlier analyses and to discuss their implications for safer sex education. The objective of the chapter is to move beyond the analysis of talk as an end in itself and to attempt a direct application of discourse analytic research to sex education practice.

## Method of analysis

The analysis of all interview data was guided by Parker's (1992) version of the discourse analytic method. The focus of the analysis was the identification of discursive constructions (e.g. of sexual safety, of condom use, of trust) and the subject positions contained within them. This is to say, I was concerned with the discursive resources participants drew on when they constructed particular versions of reality. The objective of my research was to understand the way in which discourses positioned participants in relation to safer sex practices.

Discourses are bound up with practices through the positioning of the subject (see Davies and Harré 1990, and Van Langenhove and Harré 1994, for a detailed account of positioning theory). Speakers 'take up' discursive positions (e.g. as subject or as object) in relation to other people, events and activities. There are two ways in which positioning can work. First, discourses can position subjects. Here, individuals are constrained by available discourses because discursive positions pre-exist the individual whose sense of 'self' (or subjectivity) and range of experience are circumscribed by available discourses. For example, Hollway (1989) identifies the 'discourse of male sexual drive', which prescribes a biological, need-driven, asocial expression of male sexuality. Within this discourse, the only subject position available to men is that of the instinct-driven, aggressive, sexual predator. A male desire to be wooed and seduced cannot easily be accommodated by the discourse of male sexual drive which still informs many or even most heterosexual courtships in Western society. The second way in which positioning can work is through the active and purposive uptake of subject positions by speakers. Here, individuals deploy discursive constructions which afford positionings that help them meet objectives within particular social contexts. For example, a defendant accused of rape may use the discourse of male sexual drive in order to disclaim responsibility for the crime by positioning himself as the victim of his uncontrollable biological needs (Ehrlich 1998).

To summarize, discursive constructions (e.g. of sexual safety, of condom use, of trust) have implications for sexual practice by offering a range of subject positions which constrain and/or facilitate what can be thought, said and done sexually. According to Parker (1992: 5), a discourse is 'a system of statements which constructs an object'. In order to identify a discourse, we need to establish what is talked into existence (e.g. 'the male sexual drive'), how this construction positions subjects (e.g. as driven by instinct, as unaccountable) and how it refers to (and thus depends upon as well as maintains) other discourses (e.g. a discourse of a complementary passive female sexuality). In addition, discourse analysis always requires us to think about alternative ways in which the discursive object could have been constructed. This is to say, in order to be able to identify the discourse of male sexual drive as a discourse, we need to be aware of alternative accounts of male sexuality (e.g. as the product of socialization within patriarchal society).

## Analysis

### Marital discourse

Participants framed their accounts of sexual risk-taking almost exclusively within a marital discourse. Marital discourse constructs marriage as sexually safe by definition and it positions spouses as not at risk from STDs. Being married therefore signifies a state of safety with regard to HIV. From within the marital discourse, marriage and its equivalent, the 'long-term relationship', are incompatible with condom use. One participant's answer to a question about her personal condom use provides a clear illustration of the deployment of the marital discourse: 'I wouldn't have married the guy if I'd have to do that.' Paradoxically, despite its assumptions of safety, the marital discourse also positions spouses as potential victims of HIV infection. This is because from within the marital discourse spouses have to assume sexual safety and are therefore unable to question their partner's risk status. In order to maintain the association between marriage and sexual safety, spouses need to take risks within the relationship. As a result, spouses are always vulnerable to being deceived and to becoming potential victims of their partners. One participant, Ian, introduces the notion of trust in order to justify sexual risk-taking within marriage:

> Somebody who marries, for example, and trusts their partner but their partner is HIV positive and hasn't told them, then they're an innocent victim, too, because again relationships are built on trust and maybe they asked their partner as it would be indeed prudent to do. If their partner said 'no I'm clear', then they would have to believe it.

Some participants' constructions of the married state as safe included references to safety as being 'boring' or 'not exciting'. In this way, an incompatibility between safety and excitement is implied. For example, Lee feels that her circle of friends is not particularly vulnerable to HIV infection, 'because I think unfortunately most of us are all boring and all married [laughs]'.

## Constructions of trust

Constructions of trust formed a prominent part of the marital discourse. They were mobilized by participants in order to account for the practice of unprotected sex both retrospectively (in the past) and prospectively (in the future). Constructions of trust included trust-as-security and trust-as-symbolic-practice.

Trust-as-security functioned as a warrant whereby the presence of high levels of trust within a particular relationship removes the need for precautionary measures. For example, when asked whether she had ever 'had an affair where you didn't use a condom', Tina responds, 'Only with Reg and I trust him.' Trust-as-symbolic-practice, by contrast, constructs trust as something which must be communicated through taking risks. Here, trust does not provide security; instead, it is a way of negotiating a relationship. Unprotected sex constitutes a symbolic practice which maintains the marital relationship. The use of condoms within marriage, on the other hand, would 'inject doubt' (Sam) into such a relationship and signal a lack of trust in one's partner: 'It's a matter of trust and I think if I were to start wearing a condom it would be a signal that I don't trust her and it would be a very hurtful thing to do' (Ian).

Another symbolic practice which signals trust is silence. For many participants, the maintenance of trust within their relationships required strict censorship over what was communicated to a partner. Raising the issue of sexual safety constitutes a challenge to assumptions of safety within marriage. When such talk does take place, it is read as a sign of relationship change. This is illustrated by Jane's comments about her young marriage:

> At the moment I feel like the future is pretty safe. How long have we been married, what, six months, so everything is sort of rosy and everything, I dunno, I think if things started to change we'd probably have to do some talking.

Here, talking (about sexual safety) is associated with the emergence of problems in a previously harmonious relationship. Thus, raising the issue functions as a signifier that there is something wrong in the relationship. By contrast, silence (about sexual safety) maintains confidence and trust within the relationship.

## Constructions of sexual activity

Participants constructed sex as temptation, as romance and as a male preserve. Sex-as-temptation positions participants as vulnerable to the powerful pull of extramarital passion. Within this construction, sexual desire constitutes a threat to the individual's rational agency. 'Flings' and 'temptations' are constructed as ever-present dangers which must be guarded against. For example, Jon points out that 'Everybody is open to temptation in some form or other and you only need one slip and you've got it really haven't you.' Terminology used suggests that extramarital sex is unintended, sudden and irrational (Lee: 'just one mad fling'), on a par with accidental falls and slippages (Jon: 'you only need one slip'). The term 'fling' itself suggests sudden and forceful physical movement. This construction positions spouses as objects rather than subjects of the 'fling': they may attempt to guard against it but they do not fully control it.

Sex-as-romance constructs love and passion as delicate emotional and physical processes which are easily derailed by outside interference. As a result, respondents perceived safer sex with new partners as being very difficult. Jane constructs sex-as-romance when she draws attention to the awkwardness of raising issues of sexual safety with a new partner: 'It's a bit awkward when you have to go up to somebody and, say, excuse me, are you HIV positive, when you're in the middle of a romance. Kills the atmosphere a bit.' Participants suggest that in its early stages a new relationship is particularly vulnerable, and that raising issues of sexual safety constitutes a substantial risk to the future of the relationship. Anne says, 'I mean, it's a dicey time for a relationship to [laughing] start saying, you know, hold hard there a minute [laughs], you know . . .' Both Jane and Anne use tropes which construct safer sex practices as an obstacle to the smooth flow of romance. Anne invokes the precariousness of penile erection in order to emphasize the destructive potential of condom use ('Hold hard there a minute [laughs]'). She uses the progression from sexual arousal to penetrative intercourse as a metaphor for the progression of the relationship itself ('It's a dicey time for a relationship to start saying . . . hold hard there a minute'). In this way, relationship progression and sexual response cycle are deemed to share a basic requirement for successful completion, namely the absence of interruptions to their natural progression. Raising the issue of sexual safety constitutes such an interruption. Jane's use of the trope 'go up to somebody . . . and say excuse me . . .' (see earlier quote) likens questioning a lover about his HIV status to asking a stranger the time. In this way, the emotional distance created by raising HIV with a new partner is highlighted and, as a result, a discussion of safer sex becomes incompatible with 'romance'.

Sex-as-male-preserve positions women as 'innocent victims' of HIV infection. Here, women are constructed as naturally monogamous and sexually naive, while men are promiscuous and sexually experienced. Gendered attributions of promiscuity/monogamy were not qualified by marital status; even husbands constitute a potential sexual risk to their wives. A typical list of 'innocent victims' of HIV infection includes 'babies, children, wives of, you know, husbands who'd gone abroad and brought it back, and haemophiliacs or people who'd had a transfusion' (Bea). The inclusion of 'wives' within the list makes married women the only sexually infected 'innocents'. This positioning implies that married women, who are assumed to be monogamous, have no control over, and therefore no responsibility for, their partners' sexual activities and, consequently, no control over their own sexual health. Like vertically infected babies and recipients of blood transfusions, married women cannot actively avoid exposure to HIV.

Anne's description of the 'innocent wife' as 'little' resonates with this portrayal of helplessness and passivity:

Probably one of the most catastrophic things about this is that innocent people can get so hurt, that if you've got an innocent little wife sitting at home with an apparently faithful husband for x number of years and for some reason he gets infected because he does have sexual relations outside the marriage that the wife's unaware of . . .

In this excerpt, the wife's alleged naivety, her lack of awareness of the possibility of conjugal HIV transmission, constitutes her 'innocence'. Interestingly, in three excerpts, constructions of the 'innocent wife' include references to her physical location (at home). This is contrasted with the husband's 'business trip' (Jon) 'abroad' (Bea), which is the location of his sexual infidelities. The wife's position inside the home appears to be discursively collapsed into her staying within the marriage too: the 'innocent little wife sitting at home' while the husband has 'sexual relations outside the marriage' (Anne). 'Wives' are constructed as monogamous, unsuspecting and confined to the home, and therefore inherently 'innocent', both in terms of extra-marital sexual experience and in terms of awareness of marital sexual risks. The acquisition of sexual knowledge and experience, consequently, remains a male preserve.

## Discussion

Analysis of interview transcripts has demonstrated the various ways in which discursive constructions of sexual activity and sexual safety and the discourses in which they were grounded position their users. Such positionings were predominantly disempowering with regard to the practice of safer sex. The marital discourse positioned spouses as safe by definition, which meant that talk about sexual safety constituted a challenge to the nature of the relationship itself. Those who position themselves within this discourse are required to take sexual risks with their partner in order to negotiate a trusting relationship. Constructions of sex-as-temptation position spouses as permanently vulnerable to the pull of extramarital passion and they absolve them from (some of) the responsibility for sexual infidelity. Sex-as-romance requires lovers to take risks in the early stages of a relationship in order to ensure the smooth progression of sexual relations. Constructions of sex-as-male-preserve limit women's ability to control their own sexual experiences and sexual health. Sex education within the context of HIV/AIDS must challenge these constructions if it is to be effective. Unfortunately, national AIDS education campaigns in the UK and elsewhere (e.g. Wellings and Field 1996; Iglesias 1998) have often reproduced rather than challenged them. For example, bans on TV advertisements for condoms (in operation in the UK until 1987), because they might be seen to promote promiscuity as well as the widespread presentation of the condom as an alternative to partner reduction, have contributed to the discursive construction of condoms and long-term relationships as being incompatible (see also Bolton 1992).

There are a number of ways in which sex education could formulate explicit challenges to disempowering constructions of sexual activity. These may open up discursive spaces which will allow sexual partners to request safer sex practices. First, condoms could be presented as personal hygiene items in order to undermine their association with casual sex. One respondent in the study suggested that condoms ought to be 'put through the letter box by the council, like binliners'. The objective of such an approach would be to routinize condom use to such an extent that it is expected and accepted in all sexual relationships.[2] The reconstruction of condoms as personal hygiene items could be facilitated by stressing their role in the protection of women against cervical cancer.

Second, in order to break the association between sex and loss of control, sex education must encourage an acknowledgment of desire preceding the sexual encounter. This could be done through techniques such as planning for sex and exploring sexual fantasies. For example, groups of participants could be encouraged to talk about their 'objects of desire' and their ideal scenario for sex with them (i.e. place, time, activities etc.). In addition, in order to legitimate discourses which acknowledge desire preceding the sexual encounter, participants could be introduced to relevant texts, such as the writings of Anais Nin or Nancy Friday. Following Christian-Smith (1993), Patthey-Chavez et al. (1996) suggest that popular fiction holds the potential for ideological closure as well as utopian possibility. In their analysis of popular erotic fiction for women, they found evidence of positionings which challenged traditional constructions of female sexuality as passive. Images of women seeking sexual experience and pleasure found expression in combination with more traditional constructions. This resulted in tensions between the textual tropes of 'virginity and sexual agency' and 'chastity and sexual experimentation' (Patthey-Chavez et al. 1996: 93). The texts attempted to resolve these tensions by presenting a woman's enjoyment of her sexuality as motivated by love, and thus legitimate. The tension between chastity and experimentation was mediated through the frequent use of bondage and rape imagery. Here, the woman is subjected to a wide range of sexual activities, thus maintaining a certain sexual innocence while at the same time gaining sexual experience. Patthey-Chavez et al. (1996: 102) argue that erotic romances for women have some potential for creating an alternative erotic discourse, although they acknowledge that 'so far it is only possible to assume and celebrate sexual pleasure under the cover of innocence, in a clandestine space that shores up the heterosexual order even as one of its cornerstones – the obliteration of subjective power and agency for females – is contested and rewritten.'

It may be necessary to produce erotic texts which are specifically designed to challenge constructions of passion which undermine agency for both women and men. However, it is important to recognize that in order for a text to be perceived and read as erotic, it may need to deploy established sexual discourses. If subjectivity is indeed constituted through discourse (e.g. Hollway 1989), then we would expect the experience of desire and eroticism to be bound up with established sexual discourses. Therefore, the use of erotic texts in order to open up alternative discursive spaces requires an engagement with what Patthey-Chavez et al. (1996) refer to as hegemonic discourses, while simultaneously subverting them. To some extent, erotic fiction for women, as a genre, constitutes a challenge to traditional sexual discourses because it positions women as the subject of desire rather than the object, or its embodiment (Patthey-Chavez *et al.* 1996).

Third, the close association between sex and romance needs to be problematized. As long as sex signifies love, sexual partners are disempowered. Participants need to learn to communicate their preparedness to enter into a romantic relationship in ways other than unsafe sex. The suggestion of dissociating the concepts of love and sex does not mean that we should not have sex with people we love. What it does mean, though, is that sex education needs to acknowledge that sex takes place within a wide range of relationships and settings, many of which have nothing to do with romantic love. Sex education needs to enable participants to recognize their own and their partners' needs – be they for sex, love, romance or a combination of these – and to communicate these without the help of unsafe sex. Memory work (Haug 1987; Crawford *et al.* 1992) as a sex education tool provides an opportunity for participants to explore memories of sexual episodes and to identify alternative ways in which these could have been constructed and negotiated (Harden and Willig 1998). In memory work, participants write memories to a particular cue (e.g. unsafe sex). All memories are then collectively discourse analysed by the group.[3] Following a group discussion, participants rewrite their memories in the light of the collective analysis. In this way, limiting constructions can be identified and strategies for resisting disempowering positionings can be incorporated and shared within the group.

Fourth, in order to challenge constructions of female sexuality as passive, women's active and agentic sexuality must be acknowledged. This may involve the teaching of masturbation to women of all ages as well as the use of fantasy and/or erotic imagery. Autoerotic practices, such as masturbation or the use of sexual fantasies, position the woman both as agent (or source) and as object (or recipient) of pleasure, thus allowing her to acknowledge herself as sexual subject. Finally, in order to encourage reflexivity, participants could be invited to deconstruct their favourite love song and to examine subject positionings offered by its discourses. Its limiting as well as empowering aspects could be explored.

It is important to acknowledge the limitations of these recommendations for sex education practice. First, any strategy which relies exclusively upon the modification of discourses must be limited by its inherent idealism. Parker (1992: 28) reminds us that discourses are grounded in social and material structures such as institutions, and that 'discourse analysis needs to attend to the conditions which make the meanings of texts possible'. Parker (1992: 38–9) lists the following material constraints upon discourse and thus upon discursive change: (a) direct physical coercion; (b) the material organization of space; (c) the habitual, physical orientation of the individual to discourse of different kinds; (d) the constitution of subjectivity in language. Parker argues that in all four cases, access to alternative discourses depends upon changes in real conditions outside text. Thus, when applied to the material grounding of sexual discourses, the following blocks on the development of alternative forms, to use Parker's terminology, can be identified. The case of rape will serve as an example of direct physical coercion. In such a situation, it may not be physically possible for the victim to develop new discourses of sexual agency and desire. The institutions of marriage and the nuclear family give rise to a particular material organization of space, such as single-family accommodation, which do not facilitate collective discussions of sexuality and sexual experience. In this way, the material organization of space supports a discursive construction of sexuality as private. The habitual, physical orientation of the individual to a particular form of sexual discourse is grounded in the individual's experience of sexuality. In order to be able to access new (and, arguably, liberating) discourses, it may be necessary for the individual to break from past practices. In other words, discursive change does not precede behavioural and experiential change, but is bound up with it. Thus, the sexual experiences of, say, a prostitute and a monogamous spouse may limit their respective constructions of sexual activity. The constitution of subjectivity in language and its role in the development of new discourses has already been referred to. Essentially, certain sexual subject positions have become associated with certain emotional as well as physical responses. Any attempt to encourage people to take up new (and, arguably, more empowering) subject positions will have to confront the possibility that these new positions do not mobilize the same (or any) emotions and sensations. In other words, the complex dynamics of desire cannot be ignored if new (empowering) sexual discourses are to replace old (limiting) ones.

A second criticism of my recommendations for discursive change concerns their didactic approach. Any attempt to use sex education in order to modify others' discursive resources could be seen as manipulative. If, as suggested above, discourses constitute subjectivity, then the use of education to introduce people to new discursive constructions amounts to an attempt at changing people's sense of self, rather than simply changing certain of their behaviours or attitudes. Here, the educator is using his or her power in order to reshape an individual's subjectivity. This is problematic, whether or not this power is used in order to empower participants.

Third, there is the danger of simply replacing one set of hegemonic discourses with another. Tiefer (1995) shows how Masters and Johnson's (1966) account of the 'human sexual response cycle' (HSRC), originally intended to demonstrate women's equality with men in relation to sexual arousal and orgasm, has become a way of pathologizing women who do not conform to the cycle. Thus, what may once have been a discursive challenge to constructions of women as sexually unresponsive and uninterested has become another limiting discourse of a mechanical, asocial, gender-blind sexuality.

It follows that interventions based upon discourse analytic studies need to take into consideration their own limitations and attempt to address the issues raised above. For sex educators this means three things. First, in order to transcend the idealism of a purely discursive approach to sexual change, we need actively to challenge those material and social structures which support limiting and oppressive sexual discourses. Such a challenge could take the form of participation in campaigns against laws reinforcing the power of such structures and institutions, or of community work which aims to provide organizational spaces where alternative forms of talk about sexuality can be developed. Second, sex educators need to adopt at least a self-empowerment but better still a collective action model of health education, as defined by French and Adams (1986), in order to avoid a top-down imposition of alternative discursive constructions. In practice, this means that the educator's task is to facilitate a process by which people reflexively and collectively identify limitations in their sexual repertoires (both of discourse and practice) and formulate desirable alternatives. Third, in order to counteract the process of reification of formerly alternative (and, it is hoped, empowering) discourses, (collective, reflexive) sex education would have to be an ongoing, never-to-be-completed project. Only permanent revision and subversion of sexual discourses can challenge the development of new hegemonic forms.

## Notes

1 Despite this diversification, heterosexual adults have not received a fair share of sex education. Media, research and interventions maintain a preoccupation with traditional 'risk groups', such as gay men and injecting drug users. In addition, heterosexual adolescents have become the subject of numerous studies and interventions in the field of HIV and AIDS (see Warwick and Aggleton 1990 for a critical discussion of the construction of the 'at-risk' adolescent). However, heterosexual mature adults have not been targeted in the same way.
2 A striking shift in discourse and practice in the UK can be observed in relation to seatbelt use in cars, which used to carry connotations of lack of trust in the driver's ability. Now required by law, seatbelt use has become a matter of routine for most people.
3 Although Crawford et al. (1992) do not explicitly refer to their method as discourse analysis, their use of texts and their emphasis upon the social production of meaning and the positioning of the subject suggest that memory work does constitute a form of discourse analysis.

## References

Abraham, C. and Sheeran, P. (1993) Inferring cognitions, predicting behaviour: two challenges for social cognition models. Topic review: social cognitions in health psychology, *Health Psychology Update*, 14: 18–23.

Abraham, C. and Sheeran, P. (1994) Modelling and modifying young heterosexuals' HIV preventative behaviour: a review of theories, findings and educational implications, *Patient Education and Counselling*, 23: 173–86.

Beckett, F. (1993) Sex and the secondary teacher: how to get across the message, *The Guardian*, 16 March.

Bolton, R. (1992) AIDS and promiscuity: muddles in the models of HIV prevention. In R. Bolton and M. Singer (eds) *Rethinking AIDS Prevention: Cultural Approaches*. Reading: Gordon & Breach.

Christian-Smith, L. K. (1993) Constituting and re-constituting desire: fiction, fantasy and femininity. In L. K. Christian-Smith (ed.) *Texts of Desire: Essays on Fiction, Femininity and Schooling*. London: Falmer.

Conner, M. (1993) Pros and cons of social cognition models in health behaviour. Topic review: social cognitions in health psychology, *Health Psychology Update*, 14: 24–31.

Conner, M., Holland, C., Wolinsky, A., Thompson, N. and Gilhespy, M. (1994) Challenging risky driving behaviour in young adults. Conference paper, University of Cambridge, BPS Social Section Annual Conference, 20–22 September.

Conner, M. and Norman, P. (1995) *Predicting Health Behaviour*. Buckingham: Open University Press.

Crawford, J., Kippax, S., Onyx, J., Gault, U. and Benton, P. (1992) *Emotion and Gender: Constructing Meaning from Memories*. London: Sage.

Davies, B. and Harré, R. (1990) Positioning: the discursive production of selves, *Journal for the Theory of Social Behaviour*, 20(1): 43–63.

Durham, M. (1997) Conservative agendas and government policy. In L. Segal (ed.) *New Sexual Agendas*. London: Macmillan.

Ehrlich, S. (1998) The discursive reconstruction of sexual consent, *Discourse and Society*, 9(2): 149–71.

French, J. and Adams, L. (1986) From analysis to synthesis, *Health Education Journal*, 16 August, 493–5.

Harden, A. and Willig, C. (1998) An exploration of the discursive constructions used in young adults' memories and accounts of contraception, *Journal of Health Psychology*, 3(3): 429–45.

Haug, F. (1987) *Female Sexualization*. London: Verso.

Hollway, W. (1989) *Subjectivity and Method in Psychology*. London: Sage.

Iglesias, M. (1998) 'Put it on, put it on him'. A cross-cultural comparison between discourses used in Spanish and British HIV/AIDS campaigns', unpublished MSc thesis, Middlesex University.

Ingham, R. (1993) Old bodies in older clothes. Topic review: social cognitions in health psychology, *Health Psychology Update*, 14: 31–6.

Ingham, R., Woodcock, A. and Stenner, K. (1991) Getting to know you . . . young people's knowledge of their partners at first intercourse, *Journal of Community and Applied Social Psychology*, 1: 117–32.

Ingham, R., Woodcock, A. and Stenner, K. (1992) The limitations of rational decision-making models as applied to young people's sexual behaviour. In P. Aggleton, P. Davies and G. Hart (eds) *AIDS: Rights, Risk and Reason*. London: Falmer Press.

LaPiere, R. T. (1934) Attitudes versus actions, *Social Forces*, 13: 230–7.

MacLeod, D. (1995) Family group says sex lessons encourage experimentation, *The Guardian*, 13 March.

Marks, D., Murray, M., Valach, L., Evans, B. and Willig, C. (in press) *Health Psychology*. London: Sage.

Masters, W. H. and Johnson, V. E. (1966) *Human Sexual Response*. Boston: Little Brown.

Ogden, J. (1996) *Health Psychology: A Textbook*. Buckingham: Open University Press.

Parker, I. (1992) *Discourse Dynamics: Critical Analysis for Social and Individual Psychology*. London: Routledge.

Patthey-Chavez, G. G., Clare, L. and Youmans, M. (1996) Watery passions: the struggle between hegemony and sexual liberation in erotic fiction for women, *Discourse and Society*, 7(1): 77–106.

Pitts, M. (1996) *The Psychology of Preventive Health*. London: Routledge.

SSRU (1994) Reviews of effectiveness: HIV prevention and sexual health interventions, Social Science Research Unit, Institute of Education, University of London, *SSRU Database Project No. 1*, September 1994 (revised edition).

Tiefer, L. (1995) *Sex Is Not a Natural Act and Other Essays*. Oxford: Westview Press.

Van Langenhove, L. and Harré, R. (1994) Cultural stereotypes and positioning theory, *Journal for the Theory of Social Behaviour*, 24(4): 359–72.

Warwick, I. and Aggleton, P. (1990) 'Adolescents', young people and AIDS research. In P. Aggleton, P. Davies and G. Hart (eds) *AIDS: Individual, Cultural and Policy Dimensions*. Basingstoke: Falmer Press.

Wellings, K. and Field, B. (1996) *Stopping AIDS: AIDS/HIV Public Education and the Mass Media in Europe*. London: Longman.

Wicker, A. W. (1969) Attitudes versus actions: the relationship of verbal and overt behavioural responses to attitude objects, *Journal of Social Issues*, 25: 41–78.

Willig, C. (1995) 'I wouldn't have married the guy if I'd have to do that': heterosexual adults' constructions of condom use and their implications for sexual practice, *Journal of Community and Applied Social Psychology*, 5: 75–87.

Willig, C. (1997) The limitations of trust in intimate relationships: constructions of trust and sexual risk-taking, *British Journal of Social Psychology*, 36: 211–21.

Willig, C. (1998) Constructions of sexual activity and their implications for sexual practice: lessons for sex education, *Journal of Health Psychology*, 3(3): 383–92.

# 7 Tablet talk and depot discourse: discourse analysis and psychiatric medication

## DAVID HARPER

### The practice of prescription

Psychiatry and the field of mental health in general has proved to be the focus of much recent critical and discursive research. However, a good deal of this work has focused on diagnosis (e.g. Barrett 1988), with psychotherapy being the only treatment being examined in any depth (e.g. Soal and Kottler 1996), while 'physical' treatments like psychiatric medication have attracted relatively little interest. This is perhaps understandable given the tendency to privilege the linguistic in discursive methodologies. However, such research does not adequately represent the experience of most users of psychiatric services, who often do not know their diagnosis and who tend to get drugs or electro-convulsive therapy (ECT) as a first line treatment rather than psychotherapy (Rogers et al. 1993). While critical psychologists have begun to critique the assumptions of dominant psychiatric concepts like 'schizophrenia' (e.g. Bentall 1990; Boyle 1990), medication has received little analytic attention (although see Harrop et al. 1996;

Holmes and Newnes 1996), while commentators often seem to be divided into camps seeing the case for medication as 'unarguable' or as always harmful. However, some recent work suggests that professionals and users have complex views about medication that do not fit easily into 'pro' or 'anti' categorization (Day *et al.* 1996).

The relative neglect of medication in critical discursive work in mental health parallels criticisms of health psychology in that, as Yardley (1996) has noted, social scientists risk surrendering the analysis of the physical realm to medicine. As a practising mental health professional myself, I see every day the consequences of ignoring such a realm and the difficulties progressive professionals have in countering the oppressive practice of psychiatry. It is all very well making sweeping criticisms of psychiatry as oppressive, but what practical help can we give to service users and professionals caught in the system? In this chapter I hope to develop an analysis of discourse about medication, particularly apparent medication failure, and give an outline of some practical suggestions that are consistent with this analysis. Although the analysis here to some extent maintains a privileging of the linguistic by focusing on interview material, I feel it is still of use, since medication decisions, diagnoses, drugs, dosages, side-effects and so on are not only routinely discussed in interviews and meetings but could be said to be constructed through talk.

## Locating psychiatric medication as a social practice

One popular view in psychiatry is that psychiatric treatment was relatively medieval until the development of neuroleptic medication in the 1950s, which allowed the process of decarceration to begin (Light 1980). Day and Bentall (1996) note, however, that the reduction of numbers in psychiatric hospitals was the result of broad changes in social policy and was relatively unaffected by new treatments. Moreover, they comment that the history of neuroleptics is not one of theories of psychopathology leading directly, in the laboratory, to the development of new psycho-pharmacological compounds. Rather, it is a story of accident. Chlorpromazine, for example, was originally synthesized as an anti-histamine in France and its anti-psychotic properties were only discovered later.

Nettleton (1995: 247) has noted that 'whilst care and control in institutions were described by Foucault as Panoptic power, care and control of people in the community have been characterized by what Armstrong [1983] has called "Dispensary power".' Within this form of organization, then, it could be argued that medication plays a significant role. Outside the confines of the hospital, medication is one of the forces which effects regulation by fixing patients in a diagnostic space which is not so much geographical (as in the physical separation of people in asylums) as conceptual and ideological.

Medication also continues forms of physical regulation which are not as overt as they may have been in the past (as with confinement and physical restraint) but more hidden.

Discourses about medication, like other discourses, are not just all talk. Medication has physical effects on people (although the effects will vary for a whole host of reasons) and different discourses of practice have different effects. One culturally available discourse concerns the variability of prescribing practices. Thus researchers like Rogers *et al.* (1993) have described 'irrational' and 'production-line' prescribing, 'polypharmacy' and 'megadosing' (i.e. prescribing drugs above the limits noted in the *British National Formulary*). Another discourse concerns the dangers of medication. Thus Mihill (1994) reported that one death a week in the UK was caused by psychiatric drugs, while Breggin (1983) described major tranquillizers as 'neurotoxic'. Another discourse concerns 'side-effects' (Day and Bentall 1996; Healy 1997), a euphemism for direct but unintended effects of pharmacological compounds.

Talk about medication, then, exists in a matrix of other discourses and institutional relations: for example, of medical power, the regulation of the self, the relationship between mind and body. Important in this matrix are drug companies, and Breggin (1996) terms the link between these companies and mental health institutions the 'psycho-pharmaceutical complex'. One needs to have relatively little exposure to mental health practice to see that certain discourses are privileged by this complex in adverts in doctor's journals, the sponsoring of conferences and so on. Often professionals (and, indeed, many users and relatives) get most of their information about medication from pharmaceutical representatives, so-called 'drug reps'. Greenwood (1994) comments that they do influence prescribing behaviour and estimates that there are over 4500 such representatives, making one for every six GPs in the UK – with over £5000 per year being spent on promotional material. Shaughnessy and Slawson (1996) have pointed out how much of the information supplied by these representatives is inaccurate and is even at odds with their company's own literature. Discourse about medication is, therefore, a contested area, with accounts vying for exposure and credibility, and is thus an attractive arena within which to use discourse analysis.

## On application and usefulness

Contributors to this volume have adopted different stances to the topic of 'application'. There are a number of different problems with the concept, not least that it implies a mechanistic, naive, lineal and reductionistic view in suggesting that ideas from 'research' be taken out of context and *applied* to a context of 'practice' without any problematizing of these terms.

However, I do wish the research I am engaged in to have political effects, but rather than talk of application I prefer the idea of *usefulness*. Gergen has discussed this concept further elsewhere (Misra 1993), and it links with postmodern notions of links between theory and practice (Hoshmand and Polkinghorne 1992). By usefulness here I do not mean a technical utility in the sense of developing new treatment technologies, but refer to whether a particular idea or intervention leads to richer understanding and to just and socially responsible outcomes. Of course, there are still difficulties here. For example, the concept does not tell us *who* it is who judges whether something is useful, and there is the danger, as Danziger (1997) points out, of the old wine, new bottles syndrome, where, for example, the therapy establishment assimilates useful ideas into conventional practices. This links in with Willig's (Introduction, this volume) criticism that workers seeking to 'empower' others fail to offer criteria for differentiating between differing definitions of empowerment.

I have argued elsewhere (Harper 1996a) that deconstruction in mental health is not about simplistic humanistic empowerment, but is about challenging important oppositions implied within clinical categories: individual/social; reason/unreason; pathology/normality; form/content; pure categories/messiness; and professional/service user. I have also suggested that the value of interventions (e.g. therapies in mental health) could be judged by the extent to which they challenge these oppositions, and that all need to be challenged. Frosh (1992) argues that such challenges require not necessarily choosing one term over another, but challenging the basis of the opposition, the conceptual policing that keeps the terms apart. I would agree that what I would consider 'better' interventions would be those involved in the deconstruction of these oppositions as well as those tracing the influence of power and the production of gender, race, age, class, sexuality and so on. But we risk a utopianism here and it may be that a short-term politically effective intervention might be one which champions a currently subjugated term over its dominant rival. Burman and Parker (1993: 170) note that 'discourse analysts now can champion the cause of a particular discourse by elaborating the contrasting consequences of each discursive framework, and can promote an existing (perhaps subordinate) discourse.' As we argued in Parker *et al.* (1995), there are no perfect interventions and all involve some problematic assumptions. But some are less worse than others and thus we may choose to use them to 'trouble mainstream approaches' as 'deconstructive spanners in the clinical truth machine' (Parker *et al.* 1995: 102). Such work involves tactical thinking rather than a reliance on notions of fixed truth. Willig (1997: 24) has warned that a focus only on tactics is misconceived, since 'tactics must flow from a position which itself cannot be the result of tactical choices', so when we are engaged in alternative practices we have to remain vigilant that the new practices do not simply reassert the old problems in new guises.

How can research be useful? Rather than start at the level of this chapter and see what might be 'applied', I have found it helpful to focus on particular target groups and ask what in my research might be of interest or of use to them, as well as asking what will be the most influential medium of communication for each group. Thus one might seek to influence academics and professionals through the published literature and books like this, while one might seek to influence users of services through user newsletters and meetings. Willig's (Introduction to this volume) criticism of most recent attempts to apply discourse analysis seems to relate more to the media of application: predominantly academic texts which thus focus both on a minority of those one might wish to influence and on the already converted.

I can think of two main ways in which research activity might be helpful to political intervention. First, it can be directly linked to intervention, as in the case of action research, especially where the research agenda is driven by users of mental health services. Second, it can be helpful as an ally: for example, where research findings support the views of service users (e.g. Rogers *et al.* 1993) or where it deconstructs professional views I would see as harmful (e.g. Bentall 1990). The current research falls into this latter category, and so the issue here is less about particular findings leading directly to political intervention but that future intervention might be *informed* by ideas like these. There is, of course, no guarantee that research will not be misused – thus Walkup (1994) has noted how reactionaries can be constructionists too – or not be reified (one must seek simply to be abstract enough to be useful but not so much that reification sets in).

## Theory/method

To identify some of the theoretical assumptions that have shaped my analysis it is helpful briefly to set this work in context. My interest in this area developed tangentially from some research attempting to analyse the discourses associated with 'paranoia' (Harper 1996a, 1998a). In this work, I have described some of the dominant discourses and institutional practices which, as it were, fix paranoia in place. These discourses prescribe particular positions for service users and professionals and many of these positions are limiting for users. Moreover, the way users and professionals talk about aspects of paranoia and its 'treatment' is not straightforward, but appears to serve a range of political interests. For the most part, however, these interests are hidden by the use of, for example, professional scientific language which obscures the occasioned and variable nature of discourse. Professionals and users do not appear to talk in the way one might predict from a reading of psychiatric textbooks and dominant cultural conceptions. In my work, I have attempted to tease out a number of unarticulated cultural assumptions (for example, the implied oppositions in discussions about paranoia; see Harper 1996a) and to detail the consequences these have for users and professionals.

The kind of discourse analysis I will be using here draws on Potter and Wetherell's (1987) approach, which is allied with social constructionism (Burr 1995). Space prohibits a full discussion here, but central tenets are that language is constitutive rather than simply descriptive and that taken-for-granted notions are questioned. Thus it is assumed that people's accounts are *constructed* (although not necessarily intentionally) and perform certain *functions*. This can be seen through apparent inconsistency and *variability* in talk, which reveals that speakers are drawing on different linguistic reper-toires. Edwards and Potter (1992) describe how speakers may use a variety of rhetorical strategies to construct factual accounts (e.g. the use of vivid description, empiricist accounting, lists and contrasts and so on). However, my use of this approach draws on a wider sense of effects and consequences and assumes that certain accounts may serve certain institutional interests, though again this does not imply intentionality (Harper 1996b).

Potter and Wetherell (1995) have distinguished between two types of dis-course analysis: a focus on discourse practices versus a focus on discursive resources. Discourse researchers have often tended to fall into one of these camps. However, here I will be arguing for a tactical use of both.

In analysing talk about medication, I found Edwards and Potter's (1992) and Potter's (1996) description of rhetorical devices and strategies extremely helpful in investigating what it was that speakers (including me) were doing in talking about medication. In particular, the different strategies that speakers used to construct discursive objects as real and, in Potter's (1996) words, as 'out there' were extremely important in my analysis. I was inter-ested in these strategies, since they helped me to begin to understand some of the difficulties users and progressive workers have in challenging certain practices and ideas within the mental health system.

However, I found that identifying such strategies and their occasioned use did not go far enough. I wanted to link the talk of my participants with wider discourses available in culture and in a web of institutional power. For me, a discourse analysis needs to be politically informed to be useful, and thus requires an analysis of both culture and institutional power (see Gavey 1992). A focus on rhetorical strategies alone cannot be enough, since strategies may be used differently to achieve similar effects or may be changed – witness the rise of the 'new sexism' and 'new racism'. Thus I have found an analysis informed by the work of 'critical realists' (e.g. Willig 1998) and feminists as well as writers like Foucault to be helpful in contextualizing the use of language (see Parker *et al.* 1995). In my second layer of analysis I wish to be sensitive to the ways in which talk about medication construct a number of subject positions for users and profes-sionals, while constructing a range of objects. Parker (1994: 245) argues that discourses can be seen as 'statements that construct objects and an array of subject positions, and discursive complexes contain specifications for types of object and shapes of subjectivity'.

The meanings of interventions like medication are contested and, like diagnoses, they delineate certain subjectivities. Such interventions also contribute to the construction of categories like paranoia as a diagnostic entity. The kinds of solutions offered to effect change in 'symptoms of paranoia' convey certain assumptions about the nature of paranoia: for example, as primarily a matter of social and environmental influences, of internal psychological functioning or of biology, each with its own effect – the last, for example, helping to maintain the view that 'mental illness' is biological and requires biochemical interventions (although the logic of this is flawed; see Harrop *et al.* 1996). These interventions are conveyed as forms of 'treatment', which automatically introduces a whole range of discursive positions (e.g. of illness, diagnosis, recovery and cure) and a range of subject positions (e.g. of doctor and patient). Symptoms are seen as signs of underlying pathology and the locus of treatment is seen as the particular remedy used. Alternatively, interventions can be constructed as forms of 'help' – we talk, for example, of 'helping professions'. This again sets up a number of positions: one who is doing the helping or one who is being helped (Edelman 1977). Such discourse constructs various interventions not only as varieties of action but also as particular kinds of objects and subjects.

## The study

The research I report here was part of a wider doctoral study into paranoia for which I interviewed nine users of psychiatric services and 12 professionals (GPs, psychiatrists and community psychiatric nurses). As part of my interviews I asked questions about medication. I have described an array of positions available in medication talk elsewhere (Harper 1998a), and here I focus mainly on a small section of this talk, accounts of apparent medication failure, although this is informed by the wider analysis. Limitations of space prohibit detailed discussion of the development of my ideas, methods, the process of the analysis and so on – see elsewhere for a fuller account of these considerations (Harper 1998a). (See appendix for transcription conventions.)

### Analytic layer I: rhetorical strategies and accounting for apparent drug failure

There is relatively little research on how the business of accounting for the failure of treatments is done. This mirrors the general lack of discussion of the failure of other interventions and, of course, the notion of failure is threatening to institutions which promote a self-image of expertise. Light (1980) and Johnstone (1993) have described a range of psychiatrists' responses to situations which threaten a psychiatric model.

Judging the effectiveness of medication is a complex and uncertain business, but I would argue that it is a rare event for many psychiatrists to be open about this with users, relatives and workers and to explain to them why this might be the case (though see Healy 1997 and Thomas 1997 for exceptions to this). For many psychiatrists who use a simplistic biological model the failure of medication creates a problem. If medication is supposed to treat an illness called schizophrenia or is supposed to be targeted at certain symptoms which are then 'removed', how is the fact that often use of medication is met with what is seen as little change in symptoms to be accounted for? My reading of the interviews suggested there was a wide range of possible ways of accounting for failure which were culturally available to both professionals and users:

1  The patient is a non-responder.
2  There are obviously odd exceptions.
3  We don't know.
4  Because the patient is chronic.
5  Because the patient is on too low a dose.
6  Because the patient is on too high a dose.
7  Because the patient is on the wrong drug.
8  Because the patient is on too many different kinds of drugs.
9  Because the patient has not been compliant with the medication.
10 Because the patient has been wrongly diagnosed.
11 Because some of the patient's problems are due to manipulative behaviour.

It was almost as if there existed a fluid network or a concourse of possible explanations. Rather than get into a debate about whether these are 'true' in general or in specific cases, I want to argue here that certain strategies are drawn on to construct these explanations and that, when employed, they have certain effects. For example, they warrant certain actions (e.g. the increasing of the dose of a drug in the case of reason 5) and they lead to the construction of certain kinds of identities (e.g. of the patient as 'resistant' in the case of reason 9).

In Harper (1998a) I have described a number of strategies drawn on in constructing these reasons. An important one is *symptom-talk*, which refers to a form of narrative where focus is placed on a narrow range of observable and inferred phenomena (symptoms) which are implied both to possess agency and to be 'surface' signs or markers of 'deeper' pathology (i.e. an illness or disease) within the individual, and thus draws on Edwards and Potter's (1992) 'empiricist accounting' device. Another feature is the chronicity of the illness, which emphasizes the permanence and severity of symptoms and illnesses and usually involves assumptions about the biological and consitutional origin of problems within the person. This tends to locate agency within a problem (like a symptom) which is abstracted from the person and the context of her or his life and relationships, yet projected within them. In Harper (1998a, b) I have argued that these reasons serve to displace responsibility for treatment failure away from medication and professionals on to users and the illness, and this serves the interests of the psycho-pharmaceutical complex.

### Analytic layer II: multifactorial talk and rhetorics of chronicity

A rhetoric of chronicity was present in a number of the transcripts and could also be deployed together with other forms of narrative. The following extract is an example of how oppositions can work together to respond flexibly to challenges.

Dave:     Right, why don't you feel, why do you feel the medication hasn't affected the beliefs?

Dr Lloyd: This is the interesting thing. I think because they're <pause> they're deeply ingrained thought patterns <Dave: Right>. I don't think you can any more just say they're illness-based. Their origin is illness-based but they have had <pause> their existence and their entertainment and their reinforcement by repeated thinking has had positive effects for Alan for the reasons that I gave earlier and therefore, even if the reason for the existence of the <pause> delusional beliefs is no longer there, assuming <Dave: Uh-huh> <pause> that the neuroleptic medication that affected the other things affects what lies at the bio-chemical core of those delusions <Dave: Uh-huh> they're too important to leave. <Dave: Right, right> I mean that's, that's one possible explanation <Dave: Uh-huh> I don't think Alan doesn't have schizophrenia apart from the delusions because he's on neuroleptic medication. Erm it's difficult to know now what's long-standing ingrained personality patterns and what's long-standing, ingrained, chronic, psychotic deficits and what is institutionalization from being 25 years inside <Dave: Right> erm <pause> we will never really know.

        (Interview with Dr Lloyd, consultant psychiatrist)

This account is extremely complex, combining a number of rhetorical devices. The effects which are thus achieved are varied too. First, a number of suggestions are made as to why medication does not appear to have affected Alan's beliefs. These include: (a) 'deeply ingrained thought patterns';

(b) reinforcement through repeated thinking leading to positive effects; (c) 'long-standing ingrained personality patterns'; (d) 'long-standing ingrained chronic psychotic deficits'; and (e) 'institutionalization'. These various theories are presented in a five-part list – such *lists and contrasts* have been noted to be powerful in producing factuality (Edwards and Potter 1992). This extract combines ideas eclectically from a range of theoretical viewpoints. Such eclecticism is useful since it gives the account sufficient flexibility to meet a variety of possible challenges. All these descriptions form part of an opposition of pathology/normality, in that all the terms imply pathology and deficit – a common feature of the diagnostic language of the psy professions (Gergen 1990). Thus the subject constructed here is pathological and deficient.

Terms from a wide range of theoretical frameworks are used here: sociological, behavioural, cognitive, personality and biological psychiatry. One effect of this is that even if one of these were challenged – for example, the biological model, since medication did not appear to have worked in this case – then the other candidates could be brought in to explain the continued presence of delusions. Multifactorial talk is flexible in another sense. Such talk entails the possibility of presenting the various theories as equally valid but as fixed within a hierarchy, with biology at the 'core' with other issues, such as cognitive or behavioural factors, considered to be the mere effect of underlying biological mechanisms. There is another important point here, which is how oppositions work together. The challenge to biology posed by the failure of medication, which is met by a move to thought patterns, might at first seem a progressive move from a passive biological subject to an active cognitive subject. However, in this move the oppositions pathology/normality and individual/social are not challenged, so the thought pattern is *still* seen as within the individual and as pathological. Moreover, the speaker assimilates both biological and psychological factors by making a distinction between the origin and current maintaining factors of the delusions, and this is aided by the failure to challenge the two oppositions just noted. Even when the social is acknowledged, as when a sociological term like institutionalization is used, it is used in an individualistic context, and so fails to challenge the individual/social opposition. In a sense, then, whenever there appears to be an escape from a dominant biological psychiatry view, the alternative option is already set up still to construct a pathological individual.

At the same time, qualifications are continually offered, and these include 'I think', 'I don't think', 'assuming', 'that's one possible explanation', 'it's difficult to know', 'we will never really know'. This set of qualifications has the effect of introducing ambiguity, vagueness and tentativeness. This is a useful defence, since any individual challenge can be met with the response that only a tentative hypothesis was being proposed, together with a flexible move on to another such hypothesis.

The speaker attempts to resolve the dilemma of the medication not having affected the symptoms by suggesting that it has affected the illness which is their origin, which is at the 'bio-chemical core'. This causes another dilemma: if it has affected the cause then why do the symptoms persist? Dr Lloyd then has to do some work to suggest that although the origin is the illness the beliefs persist for a variety of other reasons. If he had been offering a solely biological account, Dr Lloyd might have had some difficulty. However, by drawing on a biopsychosocial account, he is able to neutralize challenges to a biological account through the use of psychosocial theories. The separation of the notions of origin/cause and maintaining factors is useful in this context.

Gabe and Lipshitz-Phillips (1984) noted how GPs used multifactorial explanations of their patients' problems. While their analysis implied that such descriptions were simply more accurate, such accounts can also be analysed for the *effects* they achieve in talk. Multifactorial accounts warrant a biopsychosocial model of psychopathology; but while appearing to be liberal, open-minded, eclectic and flexible, they can also function in a conservative manner by relativizing challenges, and thus functioning to maintain current practice.

Dr Lloyd argues against the implied claim that medication does not work with two points: first, that the medication affects an underlying illness (using metaphors of depth common in foundationalist theories); second, by pointing to the effect of the medication on 'other things', i.e. other symptoms. This again shows the flexibility of symptom repertoires. First, depth metaphors continually offer us the possibility of knowledge from 'experts' (a form of *category entitlement*; see Edwards and Potter 1992) of an unseen realm below the surface (here, the illness) – this knowledge cannot be verified but only supposed through the use of surface signs like symptoms. Second, the symptom repertoire can meet challenges based on the failure to achieve change in one symptom by pointing to change in another symptom.

A final point here concerns one of the theories suggested by Dr Lloyd in his four-part list at the end of the extract, where he talks of 'long-standing, ingrained, chronic psychotic deficits'. This phrase is a further version of symptom-talk, where the symptom (here cast as a deficit) is given agency. However, by virtue of it being seen over a period of time it is granted some level of permanence by being described as 'long-standing' and 'chronic' and is constructed as constitutional. The use of the word 'ingrained' conveys a three-dimensional image of inscription which appeals to a variety of depth metaphor. The repeated use of these words here, then, conveys that these symptoms are to be seen as permanent, implying that they are likely to be impervious to medication. Moreover, they are thus transformed from symptoms (i.e. effects) of psychosis into 'psychotic deficits', which are seen as affecting a person's personal abilities in a negative way (i.e. as causes).

The extract warrants the continued use of medication here despite there being no change in psychotic symptoms.

One effect of the use of these resources is that the theories and symptoms are seen as having agency, whereas Alan is constructed as ambiguous: on the one hand a passive victim of biology, institutionalization and so on; on the other hand an active rational agent. One effect of this is, as noted earlier, that responsibility is located with Alan and his illness for the drug non-response, and displaced from professionals and medication, while the criteria for outcome have been redefined (a common finding in failure talk: Spellman and Harper 1996). Another effect is that by the construction of the objects of talk here as disembodied, interventions can be constructed as if they will affect only these factors rather than Alan as an embodied agentive subject.

## Implications for different interest groups

My reading of these interview extracts suggests that talk about drug treatment failure shares a number of rhetorical features and effects. I would argue that there is a need to challenge these within a number of different contexts. As a result, I have suggested implications for different interest groups. I noted earlier that I was not seeking to apply my findings. Rather, I wish to make suggestions which are *consistent* with my analysis. As a result, the implications focus less on rhetorical strategies and devices and more on the political interests and effects of those strategies.

### Workers in mental health services

Workers need to develop skills in challenging the professional mystification of medication, user-blaming reasons for drug non-response, rhetorical strategies used to construct such reasons and allied concepts like the notion of individualized pathology. They also need to support the development of consultation and partnership with users, which entails a shift in the balance of power (see Williams and Lindley 1996).

The use of medication, like other psychiatric interventions, individualizes and pathologizes, but it is not necessarily helpful to users to take a simplistic 'anti' stance on medication, since some users find it helpful some of the time. The issue is more about whether users are fully informed, have access to a range of less pathologizing and harmful alternatives (see Harper 1998a), have choice and are in control both in hospital (Blaska *et al.* 1995) and in the community. Professionals involved in prescribing and administering medications and other workers should inform themselves fully (Day and Bentall 1996 and Healy 1997 are excellent references) and explore with clients the pros and cons of medication, looking in detail at the consequences for them (e.g. on their quality of life) and the ways they and others view themselves (see Stewart 1995; Simblett 1997).

If medication is used (and the empirical evidence on outcome is variable; Kriegman 1996), much research suggests it works best at low dosages and when targeted (Day and Bentall 1996). Professionals should be more open about the essentially pragmatic nature of treatments and should give users more control as well as developing audits of medication levels and seeking users' ratings of side-effects. There should be real negotiation between prescribers and users, and workers can also be of help in assisting users to be more assertive in case reviews and reviews of medication.

## Users of mental health services

Users need to be given more independent information about (e.g. concerning side-effects) and rights in relation to treatments, including the right to refuse treatments which may be harmful. This research has shown how complex some discursive frameworks can be and thus there is a need to train users in how to deal with discourse: for example, about their treatment. Users could develop training courses similar to models of assertiveness training, where they could become practised in challenging the kinds of strategies I have described here.

## Relatives, carers and friends of users

It is important for relatives to see users of mental health services as not categorically different from the rest of us. Labelling and pathologizing a relative are not the only way to get help, and there is an onus on services here, too, to ensure they are accessible and offer a range of treatment alternatives, and do not just stress medication compliance as the only option. There is a need to develop more progressive relatives' organizations which more clearly support users' choices and which do not put complete reliance on a solely biological approach to mental health problems.

## Trainers and supervisors of mental health professionals

Training of professionals needs fully to cover medication and its effects but, more fundamentally, it needs to challenge the oppositions noted earlier, especially the user/professional binary which leads to so many professionals positioning the user as 'other' (Thomas 1997). One way of challenging this is to link professionals' own personal lives with their practice (Anderson 1995). Seeking the views of users should become a central aspect of therapy, rather than tagged on after (Epston and White 1992; Grieves 1997). Users need to become centrally involved in the training of professionals (Williams and Lindley 1996; Thomas 1997). Training could also include examination of language use like the rhetorical strategies used in fact construction: McKenzie and Monk (1997) describe how they get trainee therapists to practise identifying discourses and positions adopted by themselves and their clients in therapy.

### Academic researchers in psychiatry and allied disciplines

Academic inquiry should not be a study of either therapeutic applications and techniques or of the political interests and consequences of theories, but needs to be a study of both simultaneously. There is a need for research to be driven much more by the agenda of users rather than professionals. It is likely that the radical potential of cognitive-behavioural 'psycho-social interventions' approaches has been blunted by their assimilation into the psycho-pharmaceutical complex. Critical researchers, then, need to locate the interests that may have shaped their own research and to keep their distance from such influences – thus refusing funding by drug companies (see Johnstone 1989). They also need to take care that their research is not conducted and published in a manner which aids assimilation into psychiatry, and they could challenge some of the concepts drawn on in medication talk (e.g. 'residual symptoms', 'treatment resistance', 'chronicity'), as well as exposing some of the pseudo-science involved (see Harrop *et al.* 1996; *Healy* 1997).

It can also be helpful to focus (as this research has done) on professionals. For example, work by Cape *et al.* (1994) demonstrates that far from there being a monolithic psychiatric view about schizophrenia, there is a diversity of views about causation and treatment. Researchers could exploit such diversity and also use currently dominant discourses by focusing on issues like the *quality* of psychiatric care, using consumerist notions of choice, autonomy and information-giving. We also need to know more about what medication actually does to a variety of people with different problems and despatch the notion of diagnosis-specific drugs, since it seems clear their effects are not so specific – this entails workers listening to users about their experience of effects (Healy 1997). There is also a need to develop further less pathologizing concepts and interventions (e.g. Romme and Escher 1993).

### Political activists

The interests of the psycho-pharmaceutical complex are served by the flexible use of discourses about medication and by the existence of a repertoire of reasons accounting for medication failure. There needs to be firmer regulation of the pharmaceutical industry to reduce costs of medication and to control marketing strategies. There needs to be further action to extend users' rights (to refuse ECT, for example). More use needs to be made of the Law: for example, in suing NHS trusts that allow doctors to prescribe over *British National Formulary* limits. John Gunnell's recent 10 Minute Rule Bill in the UK, which attempted to legislate for good practice in the use of ECT, is another example. Mental health activists need to learn from other campaigns, especially about use of the media. There need to be more high-profile protests around issues of concern – such as the lack of proper audit of ECT procedures (Salford Community Health Council 1998) and of medication (Rogers *et al.* 1993). Campaigners could use direct action techniques borrowed from environmental protests and the Disability Action Network. They need to combine such protests with well argued material for policy-makers and legislators.

There is also a need for political activists to organize around the themes of exclusion/inclusion and 'othering', and to campaign against public policies and practices which serve to exclude users of mental health services. Such campaigns are timely, as the UK Labour government claims to place special emphasis on combating social exclusion yet seems likely to develop more conservative mental health policies focused on notions of risk (Bracken and Thomas 1997). Links need to be made in the public mind between social inequalities like sexism, racism, classism, heterosexism and mental health problems (Johnstone 1989; Williams and Watson 1994).

Activists need to question their own and others' 'able-minded' assumptions, which might serve to exclude users from areas of social life. For example, in relation to 'paranoia' there is a need to question the cultural assumption which sees suspicion and wariness as abnormal rather than a legitimate feeling. There is also a need to question the assumptions on which medicating ourselves is based (Medawar 1997).

## Reflections on this approach

I want to argue that my approach is relatively clear and offers concrete and practical suggestions for a whole host of interest groups. However, there are a number of potential difficulties with it. One criticism is that it follows a pragmatist tradition and operates in a tactically essentialist manner (see Squire 1995). For example, there is a lack of symmetry in this account in my tendency to focus more on the talk of professionals than of users and the implied criticism of professionals (common in much discourse analysis; Burman and Parker 1993), and I have tended to limit contradiction and variation in this account in favour of what Curt (1994) has termed a 'singularizing' narrative (but see Harper 1996a). This lays one open to the charge of 'ontological gerrymandering', i.e. following a relativist and constructionist style of analysis but then implicitly claiming that my analysis is true and refusing to see some things as equally constructed. The danger is that practical and political interventions can then become problematic: if all accounts are equally valid, how do we choose which to act on? Gill

(1995: 173), quoting Hine, talks of the danger of 'epistemological correctness' and notes that some discourse analysts seem to want to return to the kind of disinterested enquiry reminiscent of the positivism DA was supposed to be an alternative to. Certainly, the debate about 'relativism' versus 'realism' is a peculiarly academic one involving few practitioners – contributors to Parker's (1998) edited collection on this topic are predominantly academics – perhaps because practitioners are not in a position to choose whether or not to intervene, they are already intervening; for them the choice is *how* to intervene. Moreover, by setting the debate up as one of 'realism' versus 'relativism' we create an unhelpful opposition – a more helpful approach would be to look at the positions people take in particular contexts rather than talking in generalities. There are, for example, strong social constructionist versions of therapy which, although drawing on 'relativistic' positions, would still count as an intervention (Anderson and Goolishian 1992). To be useful in helping to redistribute power one needs to focus on the strategies that those in power (i.e. professionals like psychiatrists) use. For me there is no contradiction between the use of a social constructionist framework and having a political position. The charge of gerrymandering is only accurate if I claim some accounts are more real than others. I do not want to claim this; rather, I simply want to claim that some accounts are *better* than others (Kitzinger and Wilkinson 1997).

Another problem concerns to what extent these implications flow from my analysis. Could I have come up with them without doing the analysis? To some extent I could have done: much of this analysis has looked at the political effects of language and, as Burman and Parker (1993) note, often you don't have to be a discourse analyst to spot political interests at work; rather, you need to be politically informed. My implications thus focus more on this political layer but my analysis certainly brings detail, connections and surprises as well as evidence. A further difficulty is that limitations of space and book structures constrain the account, so that it seems that this analysis and its implications are obvious and natural, whereas they have been actively constructed by me. As Stainton-Rogers (1991: 10) suggests, I am not telling it 'like it is', but rather saying 'look at it this way'. So the question becomes: 'Are my analysis and implications persuasive, taking what you know of my assumptions and politics into consideration?'

## Appendix: transcription conventions

The notation used here is broadly similar to that of Potter and Wetherell (1987). Noticeable pauses are indicated by a full stop in parentheses (.), although the timing of pause lengths were not considered to contribute to this analysis. Where an interruption by another speaker is brief it is placed in angle brackets <>. Extracts are punctuated to facilitate reading. Interviewees gave their consent for interviews to be tape-recorded, transcribed and published. They are identified with pseudonyms.

## Notes

Some of the material in this chapter first appeared in *Clinical Psychology Forum*, 114: 19–21. A 'depot' in the context of this chapter refers to a long-acting form of neuroleptic medication administered via an intra-muscular injection, usually, to an outpatient, by a community psychiatric nurse.

## References

Anderson, H. and Goolishian, H. (1992) The client is the expert: a not-knowing approach to therapy. In S. McNamee and K. J. Gergen (eds) *Therapy as Social Construction*. London: Sage.

Anderson, L. (ed.) (1995) *Bedtime Stories for Tired Therapists*. Adelaide: Dulwich Centre Publications.

Armstrong, D. (1983) *Political Anatomy of the Body: Medical Knowledge in Britain in the Twentieth Century*. Cambridge: Cambridge University Press.

Barrett, R. J. (1988) Clinical writing and the documentary construction of schizophrenia, *Culture, Medicine and Psychiatry*, 12: 265–99.

Bentall, R. P. (1990) *Reconstructing Schizophrenia*. London: Routledge.

Blaska, B., Hennings, B., May, B. and Davis, N. (1995) Psych hospitalisations: what helps and what doesn't, *Changes: An International Journal of Psychology and Psychotherapy*, 13: 27–34.

Boyle, M. (1990) *Schizophrenia: A Scientific Delusion?* London: Routledge.

Bracken, P. and Thomas, P. (1997) Post-psychiatry: broken promises, fractured dreams, *OpenMind*, 88: 18.

Breggin, P. R. (1983) *Psychiatric Drugs: Hazards to the Brain*. New York: Springer.

Breggin, P. R. (1996) Should the use of neuroleptics be severely limited?, *Changes: An International Journal of Psychology and Psychotherapy*, 14: 62–6.

Burman, E. and Parker, I. (eds) (1993) *Discourse Analytic Research: Repertoires and Readings of Texts in Action*. London: Routledge.

Burr, V. (1995) *An Introduction to Social Constructionism*. London: Routledge.

Cape, G., Antebi, D., Standen, P. and Glazebrook, C. (1994) Schizophrenia: the views of a sample of psychiatrists, *Journal of Mental Health*, 3: 105–13.

Curt, B. C. (1994) *Textuality and Tectonics: Troubling Social and Psychological Science*. Buckingham: Open University Press.

Danziger, K. (1997) The varieties of social construction, *Theory and Psychology*, 7: 399–416.

Day, J. C. and Bentall, R. P. (1996) Neuroleptic medication and the psychosocial treatment of psychotic symptoms: some neglected issues. In G. Haddock and P. D. Slade (eds) *Cognitive-behavioural Interventions with Psychotic Disorders*. London: Routledge.

Day, J. C., Bentall, R. P. and Warner, S. (1996) Schizophrenic patients' experiences of neuroleptic medication: a Q-methodological investigation, *Acta Psychiatrica Scandinavica*, 93: 397–402.

Edelman, M. (1977) *Political Language: Words that Succeed and Policies that Fail*. London: Academic Press.

Edwards, D. and Potter, J. (1992) *Discursive Psychology*. London: Sage.

Epston, D. and White, M. (1992) Consulting your consultants: the documentation of alternative knowledges. In D. Epston and M. White, *Experience Contradiction Narrative and Imagination*. Adelaide: Dulwich Centre Publications.

Frosh, S. (1992) Masculine ideology and psychological therapy. In J. M. Ussher and P. Nicolson (eds) *Gender Issues in Clinical Psychology*. London: Routledge.

Gabe, J. and Lipshitz-Phillips, S. (1984) Tranquillisers as social control?, *Sociological Review*, 32: 524–46.

Gavey, N. (1992) Technologies and effects of heterosexual coercion, *Feminism and Psychology*, 2: 325–51.

Gergen, K. J. (1990) Therapeutic professions and the diffusion of deficit, *The Journal of Mind and Behavior*, 11: 353–68.

Gill, R. (1995) Relativism, reflexivity and politics: interrogating discourse analysis from a feminist perspective. In S. Wilkinson and C. Kitzinger (eds) *Feminism and Discourse*. London: Sage.

Greenwood, J. (1994) Producer interests in medicines policy: the role of the pharmaceutical industry. In G. Harding, S. Nettleton and K. Taylor (eds) *Social Pharmacy: Innovation and Development*. London: The Pharmaceutical Press.

Grieves, L. (1997) From beginning to start: the Vancouver Anti-Anorexia Anti-Bulimia League, *Gecko*, 2: 78–88.

Harper, D. J. (1996a) Deconstructing 'paranoia': towards a discursive understanding of apparently unwarranted suspicion, *Theory and Psychology*, 6: 423–48.

Harper, D. J. (1996b) Accounting for poverty: from attribution to discourse, *Journal of Community and Applied Social Psychology*, 6: 249–65.

Harper, D. J. (1998a) Deconstructing paranoia: an analysis of the discourses associated with the concept of paranoid delusion, unpublished PhD thesis, Manchester Metropolitan University.

Harper, D. J. (1998b) Discourse analysis and psychiatric medication, *Clinical Psychology Forum*, 114: 19–21.

Harrop, C. E., Trower, P. and Mitchell, I. J. (1996) Does the biology go around the symptoms? A Copernican shift in schizophrenia paradigms, *Clinical Psychology Review*, 16: 641–54.

Healy, D. (1997) *Psychiatric Drugs Explained*, 2nd edn. London: Mosby.

Holmes, G. and Newnes, C. (1996) Medication – the holy water of psychiatry, *OpenMind*, 82: 14–15.

Hoshmand, L. T. and Polkinghorne, D. E. (1992) Redefining the science–practice relationship and professional training, *American Psychologist*, 47: 55–66.

Johnstone, L. (1989) *Users and Abusers of Psychiatry: A Critical Look at Traditional Psychiatric Practice*. London: Routledge.

Johnstone, L. (1993) Psychiatry: are we allowed to disagree?, *Clinical Psychology Forum*, 56: 30–2.

Kitzinger, C. and Wilkinson, S. (1997) Validating women's experience? Dilemmas in feminist research, *Feminism and Psychology*, 7: 566–74.

Kriegman, D. (1996) The effectiveness of medication: the *Consumer Reports* study, *American Psychologist*, 51: 1086.

Light, D. (1980) *Becoming Psychiatrists: The Professional Transformation of Self*. London: Norton.

McKenzie, W. and Monk, G. (1997) Learning and teaching narrative ideas. In G. Monk, J. Winslade, K. Crocket and D. Epston (eds) *Narrative Therapy in Practice: The Archaeology of Hope*. San Francisco: Jossey Bass.

Medawar, C. (1997) The antidepressant web: marketing depression and making medicines work, *International Journal of Risk and Safety in Medicine*, 10: 75–126.

Mihill, C. (1994) Tranquillisers 'kill one a week', *The Guardian*, 27 August.

Misra, G. (1993) Psychology from a constructionist perspective: an interview with Kenneth J. Gergen, *New Ideas in Psychology*, 11: 399–414.

Nettleton, S. (1995) *The Sociology of Health and Illness*. Cambridge: Polity Press.

Parker, I. (1994) Reflexive research and the grounding of analysis: social psychology and the psy-complex, *Journal of Community and Applied Social Psychology*, 4: 239–52.

Parker, I. (ed.) (1998) *Social Constructionism, Discourse and Realism*. London: Sage.

Parker, I., Georgaca, E., Harper, D., McLaughlin, T. and Stowell-Smith, M. (1995) *Deconstructing Psychopathology*. London: Sage.

Potter, J. (1996) *Representing Reality: Discourse, Rhetoric and Social Construction*. London: Sage.

Potter, J. and Wetherell, M. (1987) *Discourse and Social Psychology: Beyond Attitudes and Behaviour*. London: Sage.

Potter, J. and Wetherell, M. (1995) Discourse analysis. In J. A. Smith, R. Harré and L. Van Langenhove (eds) *Rethinking Methods in Psychology*. London: Sage.

Rogers, A., Pilgrim, D. and Lacey, R. (1993) *Experiencing Psychiatry: Users' Views of Services*. London: Macmillan/MIND.

Romme, M. and Escher, S. (eds) (1993) *Accepting Voices*. London: MIND.

Salford Community Health Council (1998) *Electro-convulsive Therapy: Its Use and Effects*. Manchester: Salford Community Health Council.

Shaughnessy, A. F. and Slawson, D. C. (1996) Pharmaceutical representatives: effective if used with caution, *British Medical Journal*, 312: 1494.

Simblett, G. J. (1997) Leila and the tiger: narrative approaches to psychiatry. In G. Monk, J. Winslade, K. Crockett and D. Epston (eds) *Narrative Therapy in Practice: The Archaeology of Hope*. San Francisco: Jossey Bass.

Soal, J. and Kottler, A. (1996) Damaged, deficient or determined? Deconstructing narratives in family therapy, *South African Journal of Psychology*, 26: 123–34.

Spellman, D. and Harper, D. J. (1996) Failure, mistakes, regret and other subjugated stories in family therapy, *Journal of Family Therapy*, 18: 205–14.

Squire, C. (1995) Pragmatism, extravagance and feminist discourse analysis. In S. Wilkinson and C. Kitzinger (eds) *Feminism and Discourse*. London: Sage.

Stainton-Rogers, W. (1991) *Explaining Health and Illness: An Exploration of Diversity*. London: Harvester Wheatsheaf.

Stewart, K. (1995) On pathologising discourse and psychiatric illness: an interview within an interview. In M. White (ed.) *Re-authoring Lives: Interviews and Essays*. Adelaide: Dulwich Centre Publications.

Thomas, P. (1997) *The Dialectics of Schizophrenia*. London: Free Association Books.

Walkup, J. (1994) Commentary on Harper, 'The professional construction of paranoia and the discursive use of diagnostic criteria', *British Journal of Medical Psychology*, 67: 147–51.

Williams, J. and Lindley, P. (1996) Working with mental health service users to change mental health services, *Journal of Community and Applied Social Psychology*, 6: 1–14.

Williams, J. and Watson, G. (1994) Mental health services that empower women: the challenge to clinical psychology, *Clinical Psychology Forum*, 64: 6–12.

Willig, C. (1997) Making a difference: can discourse analysis Inform psychological interventions? Conference paper, Annual Conference of the British Psychological Society, Heriot-Watt University, Edinburgh, 3–6 April.

Willig, C. (1998) Social constructionism and revolutionary socialism: a contradiction in terms? In I. Parker (ed.) *Social Constructionism, Discourse and Realism.* London: Sage.

Yardley, L. (1996) Reconciling discursive and materialist perspectives on health and illness: a reconstruction of the biopsychosocial approach, *Theory and Psychology*, 6: 485–508.

# 8 Conclusion: opportunities and limitations of 'applied discourse analysis'

## CARLA WILLIG

The production of this book was motivated by the desire to explore the potential applicability of discourse analytic research. It set out to examine the possibility of an 'applied discourse analysis' through a close look at six discourse analytic studies and their implications for social and psychological practice. I approached contributors with a brief which asked them to discuss the discourse analyses they were working on with reference to their practical utility. I asked them to address directly and explicitly questions of applicability in relation to discourse analysis. Let us take a look at how each of the contributions to this book deals with the question of application.

### Orientations to application

Steven Brown produces a critical reading of stress self-help literature which demonstrates how personal distress is translated into the language of stress and how personal concerns are reconstructed accordingly. He argues that such a critical reading enables us to disentangle wider concerns and emotions from the stress narratives within which they are embedded. Brown identifies the workplace and labour relations as an important area of application for such work. A critical reading of stress literature can provide the basis for a challenge to the ways in which stress discourse is used to legitimize employers' objectives and business practices and to individualize and marginalize workers' concerns and experiences. Industrial disputes, educational policy debates and medical malpractice claims are contexts within which such a challenge may be formulated. Finally, Brown raises the possibility of constructing alternative texts about stress which connect with discourses and practices of community and care (as opposed to those of war and competition). Overall, then, Brown recommends the application of discourse analysis as a tool to challenge social practices which perpetuate and legitimate exploitation and oppression.

Timothy Auburn, Susan Lea and Susan Drake trace how within the context of police suspect interviews disbelief is used as a persuasive device which positions the suspect as accountable for discrepancies and which places 'on the record' a preferred version of events. Disbelief is identified as one of the discursive resources available to the police, which enables an institutionally preferred version of events to be produced and heard. Auburn, Lea and Drake propose that their findings could be put at the disposal of groups of people who are regularly in conflict with the criminal justice system. Gays, civil liberties organizations, animal rights activists and trade unionists, it is argued, could benefit from information packages and training programmes which would enable them to resist a positioning as offenders within the police suspect interview. Here, discourse analysis can be 'applied' through making available discursive skills to those who might need them in order to resist victimization.

Val Gillies uses discourse analysis in order to explore the discursive positions women smokers take up when they talk about cigarette smoking. She identifies a discourse of addiction whose effects are disempowering, in that it does not offer speakers positions of agency. Gillies argues that within the context of health promotion a discourse of addiction is counterproductive. She proposes instead that health promotion ought 'to increase the number of positive, accessible positionings available to working-class women' (p. 84). Having identified the limitations of the discourses which structure her interviewees' talk about smoking, Gillies recommends alternative discourses for health promotion purposes. She recommends discourses which promote more positive conceptions of the body, as opposed to those which construct the body as a dominant, controlling force (as in the discourse of addiction) or those which represent the body as a separate entity in need of regulation and repression (as in constructions of self-control). Gillies identifies a number of sites at which such alternative discourses could become accessible to working-class women. These include free gym sessions, aerobics classes and meditation. In addition, Gillies draws attention to the social structural basis of working-class women's oppression and the need for collective action and self-help strategies which are grounded in social change. To summarize, Gillies recommends empowerment through the repositioning of the subject, both individually and collectively.

Pujol conceptualizes the research process itself as a form of intervention. He argues that his analysis of a number of group discussions about 'reproductive technologies' is the product of an interaction between himself (the reader) and the text. This interaction is predicated upon the difference, and thus the distance, between reader and text, and it gives rise to something new, the reading. The reading is produced in order to challenge and question that which is taken for granted; this is to say, it functions as critique. Pujol identifies five themes which structure the group discussions and he explores the ways in which these are discursively managed by participants. An opposition between 'the natural' and 'the social' emerges as a central organizing principle of participants' talk about reproductive technologies. Pujol questions the desirability of such a dichotomy and identifies unhelpful tensions and contradictions associated with its use within the context of reproductive technologies. These include ethical dilemmas and forced reproductive choices for women. Pujol concludes by calling for the development of an understanding of reproductive technologies from within a unitary, as opposed to a dualistic, paradigm.

In my chapter, I identify positionings made available by discursive constructions of sex and I assess their implications for sexual practice. I argue that sex education needs to challenge disempowering positionings in order to facilitate the practice of safer sex. I recommend a number of specific techniques which allow participants to acknowledge desire preceding the sexual encounter, which problematize the close association between sex and romance and which construct female sexuality as active and agentic. I argue that sex education can draw on discourse analytic research by moving beyond the provision of information and by aiming to make available alternative positionings to participants. The aim of sex education would then be empowerment through repositioning of the subject.

Dave Harper's analysis of accounts of psychiatric medication failure explores discursive strategies used in the production of such accounts and their consequences for users and professionals. Harper identifies multifactorial talk and a rhetoric of chronicity as culturally available ways of accounting for a drug's inability to remove psychotic symptoms. Such constructions position the user and the illness as responsible for medication failure and thus warrant the continuation of drug treatment. Harper proposes that his analysis can be used to challenge such rhetorical features and their effects. He identifies a range of interest groups to whom this work may be relevant. These include: workers in and users of mental health services;

relatives, carers and friends of users; trainers and supervisors of mental health professionals; academic researchers in psychiatry and allied disciplines; and political activists. Harper identifies training and the development of skills as a way of putting discourse analysis to practical use. Mental health workers can develop skills in challenging individualizing and pathologizing constructions, users can be trained in how to deal with limiting discourses, relatives can gain access to ways of getting help which do not rely upon labelling and pathologizing, and training for professionals can be modified to include involvement of users and an examination of language use and its effects. In addition, Harper recommends that academic researchers take on board user agendas and that they resist the influence of powerful interest groups upon their research questions and use of findings. Political activists are urged to campaign for firmer regulation of the pharmaceutical industry, for the extension of user rights and for tighter legislation around the use of psychiatric medication.

Between them, the contributors to this book propose three ways in which discourse analysis can be 'applied'. These refer to challenge, training and empowerment, respectively.

1 Discourse analysis can be used as *a tool to challenge* social practices which perpetuate and legitimate exploitation and oppression (Brown, Harper, Pujol). Sites at which this type of intervention can take place include institutions such as the law and the media, as well as academia.
2 Discourse analysis can inform *training programmes* which make available discursive skills to those who may need them in order to resist victimization, oppression and/or marginalization (Auburn, Lea and Drake, Harper). Users of mental health services as well as those called to account by the criminal justice system could benefit from this type of training.
3 Discourse analysis can be used to design interventions which *facilitate empowerment* through repositioning of the subject (Gillies, Willig). Health promotion and sex education constitute two suitable domains for this type of application.

However, all contributions also identify problems associated with the attempt to use discourse analytic research in a 'practical' way. These include ethical, political and epistemological problems, and will be discussed in turn.

## Problems with application

### Ethical problems

Both Val Gillies and I acknowledge that any attempt to use a position of influence (as expert, as educator, as policy-maker) in order to reshape other people's subjectivities through discourse constitutes a form of manipulation. Even where the objective of such interventions is apparently in the interests of the participants, as might be the case, for example, where the outcome is an improvement in health, discourse analysis as empowerment through repositioning is still a directive intervention where one group of people teaches another group how 'to be' (more successful, more safe, more effective). Gillies invokes Rose (1989) when she agues that such interventions could be said to constitute an attempt to 'govern the soul'.

There are two ways in which these ethical concerns can be addressed. First, we need to adopt a collective action model of health promotion which provides an opportunity for empowerment through collective action. Here, discourse analysis does not precede the health promotion intervention; instead, it becomes a tool which is used by a collective in order to identify limitations of as well as desirable alternatives to current discursive practices. In other words, discourse analysis becomes a tool at the disposal of those who want to change themselves rather than a tool for the manipulation of others. Second, we need to differentiate between the perpetuation of existing power relations and the strategic use of power. Stable institutionalized power relations, such as those between teacher and pupil, doctor and patient, employer and employee, are reinforced when we use psychological research in order to ensure the smooth running of the institutions which they serve. However, forms of 'expertise' or 'knowledge' can be passed on for strategic purposes from one group of people to another. Halperin (1995: 85) cites Foucault's comments about the difference between power and domination within this context:

> I don't see where evil is in the practice of someone who, in a given game of truth, knowing more than another, tells him what he must do, teaches him, transmits knowledge to him, communicates skills to him. The problem is rather to know how you are to avoid in these practices . . . the effects of domination . . .

## Political problems

There are two major concerns about the politics of application. First, 'applied discourse analysis' appears to privilege language and to neglect the role of social and material factors. Both Gillies and I draw attention to the need to tackle the social and material structures which support discourses and practices if we want to bring about significant changes in people's lives. An 'applied discourse analysis' which does not attend to the institutional basis of discourse and subjectivity runs the risk of overestimating its ability to effect change and of blaming individual speakers for failing to shake off limiting discourses. Second, discourse analytic research can be (ab)used by a variety of interest groups irrespective of the authors' original intentions.

Auburn, Lea and Drake identify the problem of 'whom to engage with' (p. 62), and Harper wonders 'who judges whether something is useful' (p. 128). In order to guard against the abuse of discourse analytic research as well as to identify any unintended negative consequences, such as re-ification of formerly liberatory discourses, ongoing reflexive evaluation is essential (e.g. Auburn, Lea and Drake, Willig). This means that discourse analysts whose work is in some way 'put into practice' should not walk away once they have completed their original research. Instead, they need to maintain involvement with the discourse analytically inspired intervention in order to reflect upon the ways in which the intervention is changing the context within which it is being applied and how this, in turn, changes the effects of the intervention itself.

## Epistemological problems

Both Brown and Harper identify a tension between the epistemological relativism of constructionist research and the truth claims associated with interventionist work. This is to say, if discourses construct different versions of reality, on what grounds do we promote 'our' version? How do we justify our recommendations for practice if the concepts which inform such practice can, in turn, be deconstructed? How do we escape from a never-ending cycle of reflexive deconstruction in which our own standpoint dissolves as soon as we have taken it up? Both Brown and Harper advocate analytical reflexivity and a focus on the effects of texts rather than their truth value as a way of dealing with this tension. However, it is interesting to note that while Brown emphasizes that he does not claim that discourse analysis provides us with 'a single "better" alternative to the scientific approach to understanding distress' (p. 40), Harper argues that it is possible to identify accounts which are 'better' than others even though they cannot be said to be more 'real' (p. 140). Discourse analysts have taken different positions in relation to these questions (e.g. Edwards *et al.* 1995; Parker 1998), which can be glossed as 'the realism–relativism debate'. Readers are referred to Nightingale and Cromby's (1999) volume, which directly addresses this debate and explores the limits of a purely discursive analysis of social life. For our purposes, it is important to acknowledge that 'applied discourse analysis' does need to confront epistemological questions in order to warrant its recommendations for social and psychological practice. However, discourse analysts differ in the extent to which they wish to ground their analyses in philosophical as opposed to ethical and/or political arguments. In other words, some discourse analysts feel the need to justify *why* they have chosen a particular site for intervention (e.g. the class struggle), whereas others are more concerned with *how* they can help to advance a particular cause (e.g. the redistribution of power).

## What's new?

In the Introduction, I identified three existing discourse analytic attempts to engage with social and political practice. I referred to these as 'discourse analysis as social critique', 'discourse analysis as empowerment', and 'discourse analysis as guide to reform'. Having come up with our own three ways in which discourse analysis can be practically useful (challenge, training, empowerment), we now need to ask to what extent these may correspond to the three approaches identified in the introductory chapter. In addition, we need to examine whether we have been able to resolve any of the problems associated with existing approaches or whether the limitations I identified in the Introduction are simply mirrored by the concerns expressed in the contributions to this book. As a reminder, a brief summary of the three existing approaches will be presented. This is followed by an assessment of the extent to which this book has contributed new arguments to the debate.

Discourse analysis as social critique aimed to expose the ways in which language legitimates and perpetuates unequal power relations. This approach was criticized for not spelling out how such processes may be challenged and for relying upon exposure through (academic) publication as its sole method of resistance.

Discourse analysis as empowerment moved beyond deconstruction and critique, and advocated the identification and promotion of counter-discourses and spaces for resistance. A limitation of this approach can be its commitment to localized, tactical resistance and its reluctance to make generalized, strategic recommendations.

Discourse analysis as guide to reform involved an attempt to reform institutional practices through changes in communication practices. This approach relies upon the cooperation of professionals and policy-makers. In addition, it is susceptible to idealism if it leads to the expectation that communication practices can be improved in the absence of (material and social) structural changes.

Brown's, Pujol's and Harper's proposal to use discourse analysis as a *tool to challenge* social practices which perpetuate and legitimate exploitation and oppression shares the aims of discourse analysis as social critique. However, Brown and Harper also identify ways in which such a challenge may be operationalized within specific contexts. Thus, discourse analytic studies could be used by legal representatives in courts and at industrial tribunals, by campaigning organizations and reformers. For example, a deconstruction of 'stress' could be used in the courts by those affected by Gulf War syndrome in order to challenge the argument that their symptoms are caused by stress rather than toxic chemicals and that they are consequently not entitled to compensation.

The idea that discourse analysis can inform *training programmes* which make available discursive skills to those who may need them in order to resist victimization, oppression and/or marginalization (Auburn, Lea and Drake, Harper) connects with discourse analysis as guide to reform. However, while discourse analysis as guide to reform targets those in positions of power, or at least influence, such as professionals and policy-makers, discursive training programmes would be designed for use by those who need to resist such influence. Thus, instead of expecting change to be implemented from above, through modifications in communication practices on the part of, say, doctors, teachers and therapists (e.g. Wodak 1996), discursive training programmes would allow users (of services and institutions) to effect change from below.

Interventions which aim to *facilitate empowerment* through repositioning of the subject (Gillies, Willig) resonate with both discourse analysis as guide to reform and discourse analysis as empowerment. They target professionals and policy-makers in that they recommend new forms of (sex and health) education which require the cooperation of practitioners and institutions. At the same time, they utilize discursive techniques in order to open up spaces for resistance to limiting positionings and their associated practices. Discourse-based interventions which aim to facilitate empowerment can be implemented from the top down as well as at grass-roots level. An example of a top-down version would be the use of reflexive discourse analysis within a formal educational setting such as a school or college. This type of educational consciousness raising featured as one of the five strategies for interventions advocated in the pages of *Discourse and Society* (see this volume, Chapter 1, pp. 16–17). A grass-roots version of this type of intervention would be the use of discourse analytic techniques by self-help groups whose members seek to recognize and then transcend the subtle ways in which they may collude with their own oppression through discursive and symbolic practices (see also Chapter 9 in Levine and Perkins 1987; Haug 1987; Crawford *et al.* 1992).

Chapter 1 identified three key problems with existing approaches to discourse analysis and social change. Discourse analysis as social critique was criticized for failing to theorize the relationship between discursive critique and social intervention. It was argued that discourse analysis as empowerment, with its emphasis upon diversity and its commitment to localized resistance, was in danger of fragmenting opposition. And discourse analysis as guide to reform was seen as compromised by its dependence upon established social institutions.

To what extent has this book been able to address, or even resolve, these problems? This is to say, have we been able to develop a theoretical basis for discourse-based interventions? Have we formulated strategic proposals which can unify and enable collective action for change? Finally, have we confronted the question of power relations in the administration of interventions?

I would argue that there has indeed been an attempt to theorize the relationship between critique and intervention in these pages. The connection between critique and intervention is made through the concept of empowerment. While critique is concerned with the study of discursive constructions and positionings and their ideological (and material) effects, the objective of intervention is to make available and accessible alternative constructions and positionings. Where critique is about the identification of limiting and/ or oppressive uses of discourse, intervention aims to help people transcend these limitations. Thus, empowerment is made possible by critique, yet it requires the further step of subverting dominant discourses through the repositioning of the subject. Both critique and intervention share a theoretical orientation to the role of discourse in constituting subjectivities (see Burr 1995: Chapter 9, for an accessible summary of social constructionist accounts of subjectivity). Thus, our theoretical basis for discourse-based interventions is positioning theory (see also Davies and Harré 1990).

Some of the contributors to this book have also attempted to formulate strategic proposals whose applicability or usefulness is not confined to a specific local context. For example, both Gillies and I argue that particular discourses (e.g. discourses of addiction or marital discourse) should not be relied upon for health promotion purposes because they invite subject positions (e.g. as addict, as trusting wife) which are not easily compatible with protective health practices. Harper rejects discourses which pathologize users of mental health services because they limit access to treatment alternatives (as well as alternatives to treatment). These recommendations are generalizable across a number of contexts and they provide a framework for coordinated action for change; however, they are by no means universally applicable. Discourse analyses are, of course, culturally and historically contingent and for discourse-based interventions to make sense, research and application need to take place within the same socio-cultural milieu.

We recognize that discourse-based interventions which require changes in institutional practices tend to depend upon the goodwill of those who administer the institutions. Unless we find ourselves in a situation where there is a high level of class struggle in society as a whole, the use of institutional structures in order to promote empowerment is severely restricted. However, in my view it is important to make specific demands of governments, institutions and employers even when we do not really expect these demands to be met. This is because it 'puts on the record' what we think ought to be done and thereby positions those who have the power to act as having to account for why they refuse to do so (see Auburn, Lea and Drake, this volume). In this way, we can influence the agenda for discussion even if we are unable to implement changes in institutional practices. I would argue that demands for specific reforms (e.g. changes in the age of consent or changes in sex education in schools) are an effective way of putting an issue (e.g. discrimination against lesbians and gay men) on the public agenda and of creating a space for alternative discourses to be heard. Campaigning for institutional changes can itself provide access to more empowering positionings for those who take part and thus become a form of 'psychological intervention' in itself. For instance, smokers' involvement in active campaigning against the tobacco industry would allow participants to mobilize empowering discourses of liberation, autonomy and resistance instead of positioning themselves as victims within discourses of addiction.

## Application, intervention, practice

In this discussion of the opportunities and limitations afforded by the notion of an 'applied discourse analysis', I have been using the terms intervention, application and practice almost interchangeably. I now want to explore some of the differences between them and to consider their implications for our project. Harper (this volume, p. 127) points out that he prefers the term 'usefulness' to 'application' because the latter 'implies a mechanistic, naive, lineal and reductionist view in suggesting that ideas from "research" can be taken out of context and applied to a context of "practice" without any problematizing of these terms'. Similarly, Pujol prefers to talk about 'intervention' because 'application' suggests that knowledge is produced within an academic discipline and then applied to a specific problem. By contrast, 'intervention' refers to the creation of understanding in context (this volume, p. 91).

Application implies a separation of the two domains of 'theory' and 'practice', so that theory is developed before it is applied and different professionals are responsible for these two stages. Apart from the fact that such a conceptualization does not accurately reflect what actually happens in 'applied psychology' (see Potter 1982; Chapter 1, this volume), it is also undesirable. First, theory cannot and should not be developed in isolation from the specific contexts within which it is conceived. For instance, discourse analytic studies of institutional practices are often carried out by those who are in some ways unhappy with the social and psychological effects of such practices. Doing a discourse analysis is itself already a form of intervention in the sense that it constitutes a challenge to 'what is' (see Pujol, this volume). This is what makes discourse analysis 'critical' (this volume, Chapter 1; see also Nightingale and Cromby 1999). Second, a division of labour with regard to theory and practice is problematic because it encourages a mechanistic implementation which does not involve reflexive evaluation of the effects of the intervention upon the context within which it is applied. As a result, counter-discourses and alternative positionings can quickly become reified and end up as new forms of social regulation.

We need to differentiate between discourse analysis as a method of intervention and discourse analysis as a source of applicable 'findings'. I do believe that both can be useful but I would argue that the former is preferable. Discourse analysis can generate insights which can be incorporated into existing interventions in order to improve these. For example, discourse analysis of HIV/AIDS awareness campaigns can identify discursive constructions which cannot accommodate the adoption of safer sex practices and those which can (e.g. Iglesias and Willig 1998). Future campaigns can benefit from such research. However, discourse analysis as a source of useful 'findings' suffers from a number of limitations, including some of the ethical and political problems discussed earlier in this chapter as well as the problems associated with the separation of theory and practice and the division of labour between researchers and practitioners, as outlined in the previous paragraph. Discourse analysis as a method of intervention, by contrast, has greater radical potential. Here, it is the method of deconstruction and the exploration of the effects of discourses and subject positions which constitute the intervention. Fairclough (1995: 217) develops a similar argument in his discussion of 'critical language awareness' as an 'educational application of critical discourse analysis'. Critical language awareness programmes aim to develop participants' capacities for language critique. They do not provide a blueprint for emancipatory practice. Fairclough (1995: 231) argues that critical language awareness should be a resource for those who take part and that it should be 'sensitive, non-dogmatic and non-directive'. Holzkamp (1997) also advocates a form of collective discourse analysis as a way of enabling participants to identify the limitations of dominant discourses and to locate more empowering alternatives which extend their opportunities for action.

Discourse analysis as a method of intervention allows us to challenge the conceptual opposition between theory and practice. Practice is about realizing potentialities, possible futures which can be accommodated by the present. It is not about applying abstract knowledge to discrete problems. At the same time, understanding, or 'knowledge', is not uncovered but created in our attempts to act upon the world (see Binns 1973: 5). Theory and practice work together and discourse-inspired interventions can only benefit from a recognition of their dialectical relationship with one another (see also Willig 1999 for a more detailed discussion of these issues).

## Language and social change

Before concluding this book, I want at least to acknowledge the complex relationship between language and social change. Although this book is concerned with the role of discourse in maintaining as well as challenging social and psychological practices, we do not believe that language alone can drive social change. For example, talk of a 'classless society' does not do away with the systematic social divisions which characterize capitalist economies. Similarly, new 'positive' labels for marginalized and oppressed groups quickly take on negative connotations within the wider society when the objective conditions of the group's oppression are not dismantled at the same time. However, language can play an important part in social change, and we would argue that it does not simply reflect changes in social relations. For instance, new ways of referring to oneself (as member of the working class, as gay, as European etc.) can highlight hitherto obscured aspects of one's social identity and can therefore facilitate new ways of relating to others. Changes in linguistic practices are made possible by socio-economic changes; however, they can also feed back into the latter through the effects they have on individuals and collectivities. For instance, challenges to sexist language in the late 1960s and 1970s can be seen as evidence of cultural practices catching up with socio-economic changes which resulted in increasing numbers of women joining the paid workforce as well as further and higher education institutions. However, at the same time, the promotion of non-sexist terminology was also a way of changing perceptions of what it means to be a woman and thus became part of the transformative practice of 'consciousness raising' (see Levine and Perkins 1987 for a discussion of 'consciousness raising as self-help'). If discourses contribute to the reproduction of social structures (Fairclough 1995), then they also have the potential to challenge such structures.

Discourse analysts who want to make a difference do not, of course, act only *as* discourse analysts. We are also citizens, trade unionists, employees, activists and so on, and our field of political action is not confined to 'applied discourse analysis'. However, this book is concerned with the ways in which we, *as discourse analysts in psychology*, can make a difference. The recommendations we make here, for challenge, training and empowerment, are no substitute for other, more direct political interventions. At the same time, we believe that one's role as a discourse analyst cannot and should not be separated from one's political life 'outside' academia or the profession. Tizard's (1990) discussion of the link between research and policy supports this position. She provides a clear account of how political factors can impact upon the ways in which research influences policy decisions. For example, research can be commissioned in order to furnish support for a particular side in a political argument (see also Wodak 1996: 174–5, for an example of this), in order for a government department to be seen to be doing something or simply in order to delay any decision-making. In addition, independent research will only be disseminated and thus have an impact on policy and institutional practices if it succeeds in passing through 'gateways' such as the media and professional training courses (e.g. for teachers and social workers). Research findings are often misinterpreted or distorted in the processes of dissemination and application (see also Evans 1988 for an example of this). Discourse analysts who are unaware of the wider political context within which their research takes place would be unable to trace the ways in which their work is taken up and used by policy-makers, civil servants, politicians and others. It could be argued that the more distance we attempt to put between ourselves and the world of policy and application, the less able we are to control how our research is used. I return to this point in the next, and final, section.

## Concluding remarks

This book has attempted to explore in some detail the possibility of an 'applied discourse analysis'. In the process we have reviewed existing discourse analytic attempts to engage with social and political practice, and we have presented our own recommendations for discourse-inspired interventions. A number of ethical, political and epistemological problems have been identified and the limitations of the notion of 'application' have been acknowledged. Despite these, however, I would like to conclude by endorsing the project of 'applied discourse analysis', especially where discourse analysis itself is used as a method of intervention. It is true that discourses are not simply either 'good' or 'bad', 'oppressive' or 'empowering', and it is true that one and the same discourse can be deployed in different contexts with different effects. For instance, the discourse of addiction, whose disempowering effects Gillies discussed in Chapter 4, is used by campaigners against multinational tobacco companies with some success. The observation that these companies have known about the addictive properties of nicotine for many years is a powerful argument in support of claims for compensation for the victims of cigarette smoking. However, I would argue that the effects of being positioned as the 'victim' of nicotine addiction are disempowering even if they generate much needed financial support. As highlighted in Chapter 1, the deployment of a particular discourse can have short-term benefits for an individual or a group of people, while legitimating oppressive social practices in the longer term.

As pointed out in the introduction to this book, discourse analysts have been reluctant to formulate recommendations for political, social and/or psychological practice. The issue of 'application' or 'practice' tends to be flagged: that is, its importance tends to be acknowledged but its implications are not followed through. For example, contributors to three recent edited collections (Gunnarsson *et al.* 1997; Ussher 1997; Yardley 1997), all of which present discourse analytic studies of psychological, social and/or institutional practices, emphasize their potential practical relevance, but none of them spells out how exactly discourse analytic studies can inform practice (for an exception, see Yardley's chapter in Yardley 1997). As a result, it is left to readers' imagination, talents and opportunities to put into practice some of the analytic insights presented in these volumes. This may protect the authors against criticisms for the ways in which their research has been applied, but it does not protect their work against abuse and distortion. On the contrary, discourse analysts who have thought through the practical implications of their work are more likely to be able to present their research in a way which problematizes and possibly also restricts certain (undesirable) readings.

Finally, discourse analysis can also play a role in the evaluation of existing interventions. For example, Wodak (1996) was able to demonstrate that the new school partnership programme had not, in fact, led to the democratization of Austrian schools, but that it had simply mystified power structures. Thus, discourse analytic evaluation can help to expose ineffective or counterproductive programmes and to support those which facilitate empowerment and emancipation (see also Ingham and Kirkland 1997).

On balance, then, it seems to me that the risks of abstention from involvement in social and psychological practice are greater than its benefits. Even in our roles as discourse analysts, abstention means collusion with the status quo (see also Willig 1998). We need to mobilize our skills as discourse analysts in order to intervene in the struggle over how language constitutes our world(s).

## References

Binns, P. (1973) The Marxist theory of truth, *Radical Philosophy*, 4: 3–9.

Burr, V. (1995) *An Introduction to Social Constructionism.* London: Routledge.

Crawford, J., Kippax, S., Onyx, J., Gault, U. and Benton, P. (1992) *Emotion and Gender: Constructing Meaning from Memory.* London: Sage.

Davies, B. and Harré, R. (1990) Positioning: the discursive production of selves, *Journal for the Theory of Social Behaviour*, 20(1): 43–63.

Edwards, D., Ashmore, M. and Potter, J. (1995) Death and furniture: the rhetoric, politics and theology of bottom line arguments against relativism, *History of the Human Sciences*, 8: 25–49.

Evans, R. I. (1988) Health promotion – science or ideology?, *Health Psychology*, 7(3): 203–19.

Fairclough, N. (1995) *Critical Discourse Analysis: The Critical Study of Language.* Harlow: Addison Wesley Longman.

Gunnarsson, B. L., Linell, P. and Nordberg, B. (eds) (1997) *The Construction of Professional Discourse.* Harlow: Addison Wesley Longman.

Halperin, D. M. (1995) *Saint-Foucault: Towards a Gay Hagiography.* New York and Oxford: Oxford University Press.

Haug, F. (1987) *Female Sexualisation: A Collective Work of Memory.* London: Verso.

Holzkamp, K. (1997) *Schriften 1. Normierung, Ausgrenzung, Widerstand.* Hamburg: Argument-Verlag.

Iglesias, M. and Willig, C. (1998) A comparative analysis of AIDS prevention advertisements. Conference paper, 12th Conference of the European Health Psychology Society, Vienna, 31 August to 2 September.

Ingham, R. and Kirkland, D. (1997) Discourses and sexual health: providing for young people. In L. Yardley (ed.) *Material Discourses of Health and Illness.* London: Routledge.

Levine, M. and Perkins, D. V. (1987) *Principles of Community Psychology: Perspectives and Applications*. New York and Oxford: Oxford University Press.

Nightingale, D. and Cromby, J. (1999) *Social Constructionist Psychology: A Critical Analysis of Theory and Practice*. Buckingham: Open University Press.

Parker, I. (1998) *Social Constructionism, Discourse and Realism*. London: Sage.

Potter, J. (1982) '. . . Nothing so practical as a good theory'. The problematic application of social psychology. In P. Stringer (ed.) *Confronting Social Issues: Some Applications of Social Psychology, Volume 1*. London: Academic Press.

Rose, N. (1989) *Governing the Soul*. London: Routledge.

Tizard, B. (1990) Research and policy: is there a link?, *The Psychologist*, 3(10): 435–40.

Ussher, J. M. (ed.) (1997) *Body Talk: The Material and Discursive Regulation of Sexuality, Madness and Reproduction*. London: Routledge.

Willig, C. (1998) Social constructionism and revolutionary socialism: a contradiction in terms? In I. Parker (ed.) *Social Constructionism, Discourse and Realism*. London: Sage.

Willig, C. (1999) Beyond appearances: a critical realist approach to social constructionist work in psychology. In D. Nightingale and J. Cromby (eds) *Psychology and Social Constructionism: A Critical Analysis of Theory and Practice*. Buckingham: Open University Press.

Wodak, R. (1996) *Disorders of Discourse*. Harlow: Addison Wesley Longman.

Yardley, L. (ed.) (1997) *Material Discourses of Health and Illness*. London: Routledge.

# Glossary

**Key terms and definitions**

**Action orientation** (or Functional orientation): of talk and text refers to its strategic deployment in order to achieve particular social effects.

**Construction:** the process by which particular versions of reality are manufactured.

**Critical psychology:** *deconstructs* psychological discourses.

**Critical reading:** examines how facts are *constructed* in a text, whose interests such *constructions* may serve and what its social consequences may be.

**Deconstruction:** the process by which the categories and strategies which produce particular versions of reality are identified and thus problematized.

**Discourse:** a loose network of terms of reference which *construct* a particular version of events and which *position* subjects in relation to these events.

**Discourse analysis:** the process by which strategies of meaning *construction* are made visible. DA is concerned with the ways in which language *constructs* objects, subjects and experiences.

**Discursive construction**: a way of talking into existence a particular subject or object. A discursive *construction* is more specific and more narrowly focused than a *discourse*. It can form part of a discourse but does not, on its own, constitute a discourse.

**Discursive practices**: habitual and/or institutionalized ways of talking and acting which *construct* and support a particular version of events with some consistency.

**Discursive resources**: terms of reference and linguistic strategies available to speakers.

**Epistemology**: is concerned with how our knowledge of the world may be produced, i.e. how we come to know things.

**Narrative**: an account of an event or a sequence of events which has a temporal structure and which obeys certain narrative conventions such as how details are to be described, how the presence of the author is to be denoted and the manner in which the audience is required to treat the narrative.

**Ontology**: is concerned with the nature of the world, i.e. what 'is'.

**Positioning**: the process by which *subject positions* are mobilized through talk.

**Reflexivity**: an awareness of our own contribution to the *construction* of meanings and the impossibility of conducting research whilst remaining 'outside of' one's subject matter.

**Reification**: the process by which ways of categorizing and ordering the social world through language come to act upon the world in such a way that they begin to constitute material reality.

**Social constructionism**: argues that human experience is mediated historically, culturally and linguistically. It can never be a direct reflection of environmental conditions but must be understood as a (socioculturally) specific reading of these conditions.

**Subjectivity**: refers to our sense of self, including intentionality, reflexive self-awareness, autobiographical memories, i.e. a sense of who we are and where we are going.

**Subject positions**: are 'ways of being' afforded by discourses. Terms of reference which *construct* subject positions in Western culture are frequently concerned with agency and responsibility.

\* Italicized terms are those which are defined elsewhere in the glossary.

# Index